BUILDING BERLIN

THE LATEST ARCHITECTURE IN AND OUT OF THE CAPITAL

Whose job is it to promote high-quality architecture?

Over the last few years, Germany has upped the ante a little when it comes to creating an attractive built environment. We now have the Bundesstiftung Baukultur, the federal built environment trust. We have the Deutsche Architekturpreis, awarded jointly by the Federal Chamber of Architects and the construction ministry. Every couple of years, international construction exhibitions serve as showcases for architecture's cultural contribution, and many state ministries are working with their local chambers of architects on similar projects. The federal government, too, is making its own contribution to the built environment in the form of urban development subsidies.

But whether in architecture, urban planning, landscape architecture or interior design, the lion's share of the work is being done by the creative people on the ground. On a daily basis, they highlight the importance of the built environment by submitting competition entries with no financial benefit to themselves. The chambers of architects contribute their members' resources and commitment. But other areas of culture, such as the visual arts, music and theatre, receive much more generous government support.

You wouldn't think so, given the high-quality results they achieve, of which this book is but one example. This is because people working in the field of architecture have such immense drive, initiative, and personal commitment, as you'll see from the projects presented here. The one thing they all share is a delight in designing and building things, and it's often their commitment that gets projects off the ground in the first place.

Our members in architectural firms of all shapes and sizes, in institutions and in government bodies are fighting for a high-quality built environment. They can never have too much support in this endeavour, both from the authorities, whose role extends far beyond being a client, and from the public at large. When the two work hand in hand, they create an environment in which ideas can flourish, quality is built in to everything we do, and everyone benefits.

Dipl.-Ing. Christine Edmaier
President of the Berlin Chamber of Architects

Residential

Office, Commerce & Trade

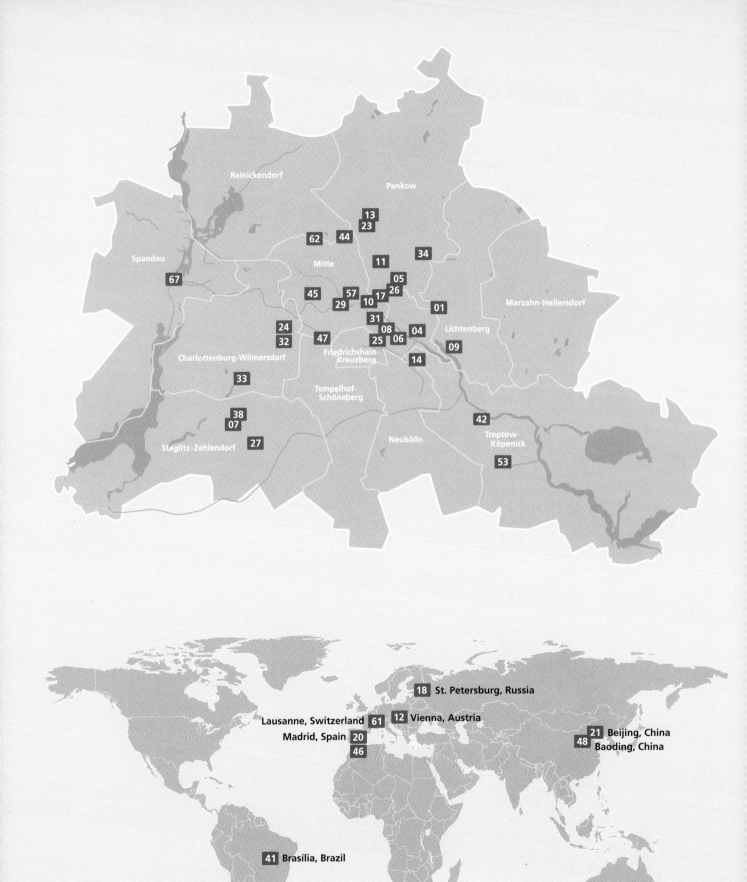

Reinickendorf

Pankow

13
23

62 **44**

Mitte

11

34

Spandau

05
26

67

45 **57**
29 **10** **17**

01

Marzahn-Hellersdorf

31

24
32 **47**

08
25 **06** **04**

Lichtenberg

09

14

Charlottenburg-Wilmersdorf

Friedrichshain-
Kreuzberg

33

Tempelhof-
Schöneberg

42

Treptow-
Köpenick

38
07

27

Neukölln

53

Steglitz-Zehlendorf

18 St. Petersburg, Russia

Lausanne, Switzerland **61** **12** Vienna, Austria

Madrid, Spain **20**

21 Beijing, China
48 Baoding, China

46

41 Brasília, Brazil

Projects in and from Berlin

This book presents 67 projects by members of Berlin's Chamber of Architects completed in Berlin and further afield prior to summer 2015. The collection encompasses works of architecture, interior design, landscape architecture and urban planning. This selection was curated by a panel of seven experts: Professor of Architecture Carlo Baumschlager of Dornbirn (Austria); Volker Auch-Schwelk, architect and urban planner for consultants *sustainable strategies* of Stuttgart; Gerold Reker, President of the Rhineland-Palatinate Chamber of Architects; Sabine Feldmann, urban planner of Düsseldorf; Irene Burkhardt, landscape architect of Munich; Hamburg-based interior architect and BDIA Regional Chairman, Nikolaus Börn; and Sascha Hingst, editor and television presenter.

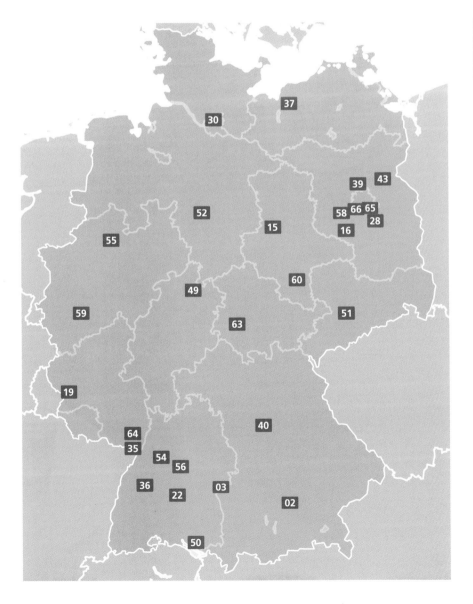

01 to 16 Residential
17 to 29 Office, Commerce & Trade
30 to 31 Transportation & Infrastructure
32 to 41 Health, Leisure & Social Services
42 to 53 Education & Science
54 to 58 Culture
59 to 65 Open Space
66 to 67 Urban Planning

Listed building projects
08 09 10 12 14 17 19 23
25 27 32 34 42 43 44 54
57 59 62 67

Sustainable building projects
01 03 04 05 15 16 23 29
42 43 46 66

Interior & exhibition design
11 12 15 18 19 22 27 45
56 57

Cooperative housing groups
05 06

Completed competition projects
02 03 30 35 40 46 49 50
53 55 59 60 63 64

Living XS

Berlin tests the new compact class

MINIMALRAUM residential experiment – this 30 m² unit in the Plattenpalast in Berlin-Mitte was designed by wiewiorra hopp schwark architekten (left), poster by Hans Leistikow for the International Design Exhibition at the 1929 CIAM Conference (above)

Averaging 45 square metres of floor area per capita, Germans now enjoy more living area than ever. And according to the Federal Institute for Research on Building, Urban Affairs and Spatial Development this figure will continue to grow. This development is underpinned by two long-term trends: shrinking average household sizes and the growing number of households overall – resulting in an increased demand for apartments. Already, single and two-person households make up around seventy percent of the 37.4 million households in Germany. In larger cities this group accounts for over eighty percent of all households. And this development has placed increasing pressure on housing markets in metropolitan areas.

While the number of inhabitants in rural areas continues to decline and available residential capacities grow, the so-called Big Seven – Munich, Berlin, Hamburg, Frankfurt, Stuttgart, Cologne and Düsseldorf – have experienced constant – and at times rapid – growth over the last decade, while actual floor area per capita has stagnated and in some cases shrunk. Average income-earners looking for apartments in these cities, particularly within the inner city, have little choice but to compromise on floor space. For many, abundant floor space was until recently a non-negotiable criterion, but in the major metropolitan areas desperate apartment hunters are not the only ones now adopting a more pragmatic approach to this matter. The real estate industry has come to appreciate that an exclusive focus on lofts would not only fail to meet the current demand, but would ignore opportunities to deliver higher returns on investment in housing.

In the dialectics of necessity and virtue, project developers have taken to re-branding apartments of a modest size as trendy *Micro Apartments*, *Smartments* or *Minimal Homes* – with all the mod-cons of contemporary living delivered in an intelligent and sophisticated architectural solution on the smallest possible floor space. The logic is simple: compact units achieve a higher per square metre price than spacious apartments.

The units are modelled after apartments built in the densely populated mega-cities of Asia. There, the challenge of creating comprehensive living solutions for even the smallest of areas has long been a concern of architectural practice. The Japanese metropolis of Tokyo, for example, is home to 14,814 inhabitants per square kilometre. Accordingly, the average four-person family makes do with a mere 50 square metres. This environment calls for designs and fixtures that combine functionality and storage solutions in a manner that facilitates everyday living. To this end interior designers make use of sliding elements, split levels, wall closets, fold-out elements and below-floor storage solutions to save space; windows, light colours and clear lines create a sense of spaciousness.

These principles have also been adopted by a project launched through the *Making Room* initiative of the Citizens Housing and Planning Council in New York. The lack of affordable smaller sized apartments in the "Big Apple" (10,560 inhabitants per square kilometre) is dramatic and regulations stipulating a minimum floor space of

37 square metres per unit for new construction projects have compounded the problem. In 2012 the municipal authorities, keen to identify new solutions, staged the inaugural *adAPT NYC* competition for Manhattan's first micro-apartment block. The winning design – *My Micro NY* by nARCHITECTS – features a modular high-rise building containing 55 units. Equipped with fitted wardrobes and cupboards, storage solutions beneath a three-metre-high ceiling and large sliding glass front opening onto a balcony, the apartments combine living, sleeping, cooking and sanitary facilities on a footprint of just 23 to 28 square metres. The inhabitants share the use of a number of rooms, including a rooftop terrace, an on-site gym, bicycle parking and storage facilities, a community room and a small lounge. Of course, living in such small spaces requires not only a certain willingness to downsize one's household and make do with less personal space, but also the recognition that some everyday activities such as laundry washing or receiving visitors will have to take place outside the home. Unsurprisingly, this style of housing tends to be more popular among highly mobile, urban professionals whose primary requirement is for a place to sleep. After all, an abundance of services and spaces for dining, leisure and socialising is available just outside in the surrounding city. The question of whether to spend money on renting and maintaining a large, representative apartment when much of our time is spent outside the home is not simply one of economics – sustainability also factors into the equation. Compact living solutions deliver savings in terms of energy, space and material resource use.

But is this renewed interest in XS living solutions driven by more than budgetary constraints? With demand for sprawl-ing premium segment apartments on the wane, a significant number of architects are experimenting with designs for small spaces and revisiting the age-old question of precisely how much space we need to live. As early as 1929 architects at the CIAM congress in Frankfurt turned the spotlight on minimum subsistence level housing. Then, experts concluded that at minimum a household should occupy a 38-square-metre unit, featuring a 14-square-metre living area with a kitchenette and two small rooms of eight square metres each. When Renzo Piano – an architect not known for humility – turns his attention to the theme of absolute necessity, his focus is not on the needs of low-income families but on sustainable designs with a spiritual value. His project *Diogene* – a prototype micro-house built on the Vitra Campus in Basel – had its roots in his desire to create a space for life's most essential aspects. The building has a footprint of 2.4 x 3 metres, a ridge height of 3.2 metres, and is made entirely of wood, with exterior aluminium panelling. The interior is divided into an area fitted with a sofa bed, folding table and chair; a shower, an eco-toilet and a tiny kitchenette are located behind a partition. As a 21st-century translation of the Vitruvian hut, *Diogene* may be simple in form, but it is equipped with solar panels, photovoltaic cells, a rainwater tank and a composting toilet. Originally, Piano had intended to design a house that could be built anywhere, at any time, without the support of external infrastructure.

And while Piano's prototype was conceived as a pioneer project, developers are already promoting XS living solutions outside the student market – now also in Berlin. At present there is an acute shortage of housing in central locations in

My Micro NY by nARCHITECTS: artist's impression of construction (left), and units in preparation (right), the former Postscheckamt Building in Berlin-Kreuzberg (below)

the German capital (3,887 inhabitants per square kilometre). Within the space of a few years the city's brownfield sites, wastelands and empty plots have become premium real estate and now trade at high prices. The planning and construction of compact, sophisticated apartments has become an accordingly profitable venture.

The forty-six apartments built on the two upper floors of the former Hertie department store in the district of Moabit reflect this development. The building was renovated according to a design from the Berlin office of architect Thomas Müller. Ranging from forty to seventy square metres in size, the apartments are not entirely deserving of the prefix "micro", but their compact spatial organisation and functional design anticipates a project soon to be realised in the former Post-scheckamt Building in Kreuzberg. The striking high-rise building, constructed from 1965 to 1971 according to plans by Prosper Lemoine, is to accommodate 320 apartments measuring 46 to 60 square metres following the departure of Deutsche Postbank at the end of 2016. The target group: mobile professionals. Depending on the purchaser's budget and specific requirements, the apartments will be made available as partially or fully furnished units, complete with cutlery and other essentials. The design, presented by Berlin architect Eike Becker, also features additional common areas, including co-working offices, a restaurant, lounge, fitness rooms, rooftop

terrace and small shops. However, these amenities come at a cost, with rents well above the city's average. The residential high-rise tower, promoted under the name of *Vertical Village*, will form the centrepiece of a new district that will feature both spacious family apartments alongside apartments suitable for students and publicly-funded housing for low-income households. On completion the development will cover four hectares of prime real estate, putting the project on a scale that investors in Tokyo or Manhattan can only dream of, where compact-class apartments are a bitter necessity rather than a trendy luxury.

Low-energy Building in the Samariter Neighbourhood

Pettenkoferstrasse 12–15
10247 Berlin

GFA 14,725 m²
GV 53,300 m³

HKA Hastrich Keuthage Architekten BDA
www.hka-architekten.de

Client: Archigon Projektentwicklung
und Baubetreuung GmbH

View of courtyard and garden building

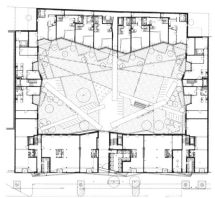

Ground floor plan

New construction of a residential complex on a 70-metre-wide empty site on Berlin's suburban railway ring. Apartments are oriented toward the water feature in the spacious garden courtyard formed by the building's four wings. Bays capture the sun and open up views along the street from the front building. Parts of the upper floors facing the courtyard are set back, resulting in wide terraces. All of the apartments in the garden building alongside the tracks and the side wings have balconies, terraces or loggias facing the courtyard. The building's primary energy consumption is 45% lower than required by German law. Outstanding insulation, efficient building services and decentralised living area ventilation with heat recovery made this possible.

Street elevation (above), maisonette and balcony (below)

Funkkaserne Nord Residential Neighbourhood, WA 1+2

| Max-Bill-Strasse 11–53 | GFA 31,800 m² | **léonwohlhage** | | Client: GEWOFAG Wohnen GmbH |
| 80807 Munich | GV 122,000 m³ | www.leonwohlhage.de | | |

View from the west

Courtyard

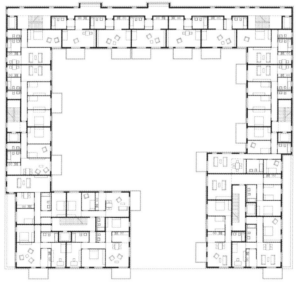
Upper floor plan

Site plan

New construction of 270 mostly subsidised apartments as the result of a competition in 2012. The project is part of a new residential neighbourhood on former military sites. The first four structures (WA 1+2) are situated on the busy Frankfurter Ring road. For this reason their north façades have relatively few openings. This side is mainly occupied by hallways that frequently widen into bays. The apartments all have a southerly orientation toward landscaped courtyards. The number of storeys in the open blocks is reduced on the courtyard side. This gradation leads over to the freestanding buildings that will be built to the south. To the east, a new building containing student and nursing care apartments, a children's day care facility and a family centre, complements the row of buildings. Transparent barriers fill the gaps between the buildings to provide the neighbourhood with even more protection from traffic noise.

View from the south (above), north side on the Frankfurter Ring (below)

Jules et Jim – Promenade Sociale

Künetteweg 5–7
89231 Neu-Ulm

GFA 5,725 m²
GV 13,000 m³

Kleine Metz Architekten
www.kleinemetz.de

Client: NUWOG Wohnungsgesellschaft
der Stadt Neu-Ulm GmbH

View from the roof of the extension

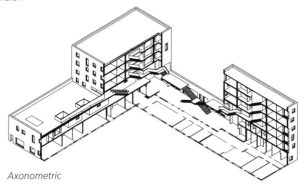

Axonometric

Staircase

New building with 31 apartments and children's day care facility as the result of a competition in 2010. The building rises to three different heights from an angled floor plan. A single-storey plinth for the children's day care facility connects the two six-storey residential towers. One of the towers transitions into a two-storey extension. So the building mediates between the fragmented developments in the surrounding area. Twelve apartment types create a wide range of options on any individual floor for all age groups and living circumstances. Broad stairways, foyers on each floor and the roof terrace over the day care facility form a three-dimensional promenade sociale – a succession of semi-public spaces for neighbourly contact. The Supreme Building Authority of the State of Bavaria supported this model project for family-oriented living in the inner city. The annual primary energy consumption amounts to 26.1 kWh/m².

View with roof terrace

Apartment Building at Libauer Strasse 13

Libauer Strasse 13　　GFA 1,400 m²　　**welter+welter architekten BDA**　　Client: Li.BAU.13. GmbH
10245 Berlin　　　　　GV　4,550 m³　　www.welterwelter.com

Courtyard

Terraces overlooking courtyard

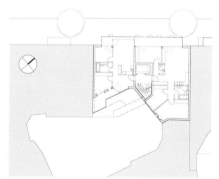

Fourth floor plan

New seven-storey apartment building on a narrow gap site. The façade picks up on elements from the adjacent building, which was designed by the same office. Continuous balconies and vertical supports for climbing plants dominate the street elevation. Stacked bays and terraces shape the plastered courtyard façade and provide every apartment with an outdoor area wide enough to be furnished. All ten apartments are barrier free, with floor level showers. A hair salon and communal garage that both extend to the basement level were developed on either side of the street level courtyard passage. The annual primary energy requirement amounts to 41 kWh/m².

View from the street (above), balustrades with climbing plant supports and apartment (below)

cb19

Christburger Strasse 19	GFA 3,700 m²	**zanderroth architekten**	Client: Baugemeinschaft
10405 Berlin	GV 13,300 m³	www.zanderroth.de	Christburger Strasse 19 GbR

View from the window

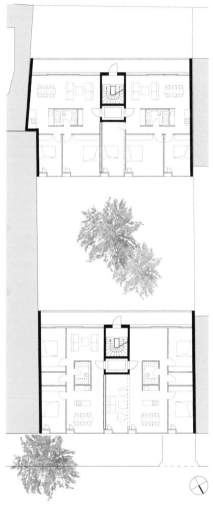

Standard floor plan

New construction of two apartment buildings for a cooperative housing group on a deep vacant site in the Prenzlauer Berg district. The six-storey buildings – each with an additional penthouse floor – stand at opposite ends of a courtyard. A common basement connects them. Thanks to long-span slabs, the residential levels have no need for loadbearing interior walls or columns. This allowed the floor plans on each level to be individually designed in accordance with the occupants' wishes. The north façades are characterised by floor-to-ceiling glazing. The south elevations have continuous balconies that are also part of the escape route network, in the event of a fire. The buildings conform to the KfW-70 energy standard. A combined heat and power plant provides heat. Hot water supply is decentralised.

View from the street (above), penthouse apartment and view of courtyard from front building (below)

Apartment Building at Wrangelstrasse 11

Wrangelstrasse 11	GFA 1,375 m²	**Schenk Perfler Architekten GbR**	Client: Bauherrengemeinschaft Plan 6 GbR
10997 Berlin	GV 4,625 m³	www.sparch.de	

Dining area

View from the street

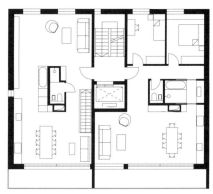

Examples of upper floor plans

New construction of a multifamily building with six apartments for a co-operative housing group in Berlin's Kreuzberg district. People from all age groups live in the building. The floor plans are individually designed. The apartments are largely barrier-free and all have a south-facing balcony (or a terrace) overlooking the garden. Exterior curtains made from awning fabric provide shade and thermal protection for both the rooms and their outdoor seating areas. The residents share the garden and the intensively landscaped roof terrace. The building is heated by a leased, mini combined heat and power plant (Lichtblick ZuhauseKraftwerk). The annual energy requirement is 30.8 kWh/m².

View from the courtyard

Fünf Morgen – Dahlem Urban Village

Marshallstrasse 8–10
14169 Berlin

GFA 7,850 m²
GV 25,500 m³

Eller + Eller Architekten
www.eller-eller.de

Client: STOFANEL Investment AG

Twin Villa III

Suite House floor plan, standard floor

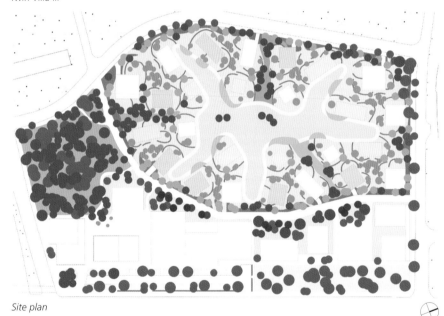

Site plan

First building phase of a car-free housing estate on a five-hectare site that was used by the United States military until the 1990s. The project is based on a master plan by Wiel Arets Architects. A total of about 130 residential units will be built. Free-standing villas, double villas and apartment buildings will be loosely grouped around an almost completely natural lake. The building types are differentiated by the design of their plaster and brick façades. They are planted in a landscaped park that replicates the vegetation of the Berlin-Brandenburg lakeland. The annual primary energy requirement averages 53.9 kWh/m². The project received a silver certification from the German Sustainable Building Council and was awarded the 2012 European Property Award.

Suite House I and Villa 5M

Taut-Haus am Engelbecken

| Engeldamm 70 | GFA 11,575 m² | ingenbleek GmbH | Client: Taut-Haus am Engelbecken GmbH |
| 10179 Berlin | GV 64,125 m³ | www.office33.de | |

View from the street

View from the courtyard

Conversion of an administrative building to residential use. The listed building now contains 54 apartments and three commercial units. Designed by Bruno and Max Taut, this corner building was erected between 1927 and 1932 as a trade union building. Later, it stood directly adjacent to the Berlin Wall. It is an outstanding example of 1920s architecture. The substance of the building was repaired during the conversion. Interventions, such as installation of an additional staircase and lift, only took place when they were essential for the new residential use. Building components, such as hot-riveted steel columns, beams, concrete and masonry, were exposed in places as witnesses to the steel skeleton structure. New awning windows on the street frontage and balconies overlooking the courtyard enhance the apartments. Up-to-date insulation was installed at the roof and courtyard façades.

Living area (above), exposed steel column (lower left), apartment floor plan (lower right)

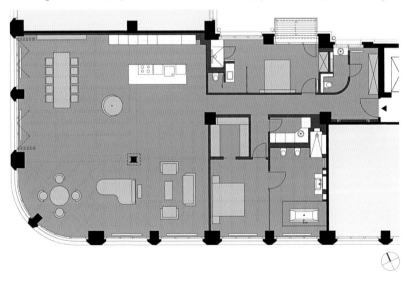

Rummelsburg Imperial Workhouse

Friedrich-Jacobs-Promenade 3
Karl-Wilker-Strasse 11
10317 Berlin

GFA (new building) 400 m²
GFA (existing structure) 1,825 m²
GV (new building) 1,400 m³
GV (existing structure) 5,700 m³

AFF architekten
www.aff-architekten.com

Client: Hauptstrasse 8 GbR

View from the east

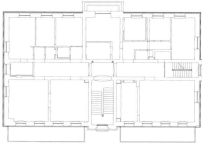

Roof level (top) and upper floor plans

Conversion of an administrative building to residential use with seven apartments. The building is part of the listed workhouse on the Rummelsburg Lake. The ensemble was erected between 1877 and 1879 to a design by Hermann Blankenstein. It served as a prison during the East German regime. The former administrative building was renovated in accordance with conservation guidelines. The portal façade on the north side now presents its original elevation again. Filigree steel balconies complete the image on the south elevation. Two garden pavilions in terra cotta coloured concrete were created in front of this elevation. Three new terraces were developed on the south side of the restructured roof. One is for the rooftop apartment and two for the maisonettes that have main rooms on the floor below.

Roof terrace (above), portal façade (below)

Neue Schönhauser 15

Neue Schönhauser	GFA (new building)	305 m²	**nps tchoban voss GmbH & Co. KG**	Client: Prime Development
Strasse 15	GFA (existing structure)	1,725 m²	www.nps-tchoban-voss.de	Property GmbH
10178 Berlin	GV (new building)	910 m³		
	GV (existing structure)	6,325 m³		

Apartment

Extension in the courtyard

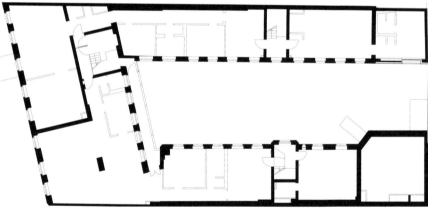

First floor plan

Site plan

Conversion of a baroque tenement. The oldest parts of the building date back to the period around 1755. Later, it was repeatedly remodelled and wings were added. In the current project, the display windows on the street were enlarged and the dormer windows facing the street were rebuilt. With the exception of the listed staircases, the interior spaces were gutted. Apartments with a new layout that incorporated the former attics were created on the upper levels. A penthouse, an extension to one wing and an installation in the courtyard passageway were added. To enlarge the retail spaces, all of the basement walls were underpinned, the basement floor was lowered by more than one metre and the courtyard was undercut. The resulting basement now enlarges the shops with a spacious second level.

View from the street (above), courtyard with historic access balconies (below)

Loft G63

10437 Berlin	GFA 150 m² GV 500 m³	**TRU Architekten und Generalplaner GmbH** www.truarchitekten.de	Client: private

Bathroom

View toward the foyer

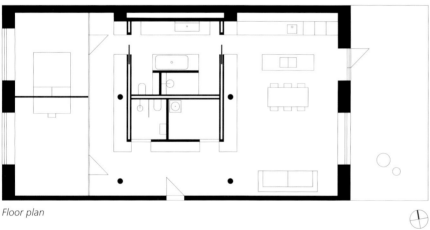

Floor plan

Conversion and development of a factory floor into a residential loft in the Prenzlauer Berg district. To retain the open character of the space, bathroom and toilet were screened off in the centre of the loft. The exterior faces of the resulting cube contain wardrobes, shelves or niches. The kitchen/living room, with counter, kitchen island and dining area, is located between the window wall and the cube. The vocabulary of wood-veneered and white surfaces creates a bright, warm atmosphere in the apartment.

Cube (above) and dining area (below)

Wohnung S

1130 Vienna (Austria) GFA 205 m² **IFUB*** Client: private
GV 720 m³ www.ifub.de

Pull-out pantry in the kitchen hall

Kitchen island

Floor plan

Renovation, redesign and reorganisation of an owner-occupied apartment.
The apartment occupies the entire mezzanine of a 1931 art deco villa in Vienna's 13th district. A vestibule, the old narrow kitchen and a servant's room now form the new kitchen. This was made possible by removal of two interior walls. Otherwise the floor plan is unchanged. As much of the substance as possible was preserved in the furnishing: windows, floors and built-in cabinets were refurbished, old tiles were laid in a new location and building services were renewed. A gas condensing boiler is now the key energy supply component. The aesthetic preferences of the owners – as varied in nature as the former German parliament in Bonn, the film *Metropolis* or old train compartments – provided starting points for the general design overhaul.

View from the kitchen to the dining room (above), foyer, living room, bathroom (below)

House in Berlin-Pankow

13187 Berlin	GFA 640 m²	**Code of Practice**	Client: private
	GV 2,600 m³	www.codeofpractice.de	

View from the street

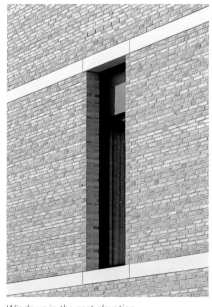

Windows in the east elevation

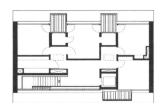

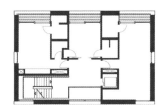

Second, first, ground
and basement floor plans
(from top to bottom)

New villa construction in a park-like setting on the Panke River. The three-storey building was erected at the transition from the villa development of the former East German embassy quarter to a taller, block perimeter structure. Kitchen, dining and living area line the west wall on the ground floor. They can be opened up to the garden with sliding doors. Children's and guest rooms are on the next floor and the parents' studies and bedroom are on the top floor. Thanks to clear-span slabs, there are no loadbearing walls in the interior. This will allow later adjustment of the floor plans. The basement provides space for a pool and sauna, a fitness room and ancillary rooms. The heating concept combines geothermal heat for the basic supply, a gas condensing boiler for peak loads, a solar system and an exhaust system with heat recovery.

View from garden (above), hall (below)

Coach House in Alt-Treptow

Karl-Kunger-Strasse 47–48
12435 Berlin

GFA 190 m²
GV 925 m³

TRU Architekten und Generalplaner GmbH
www.truarchitekten.de

Client: private

Living room on the first floor

Exterior view

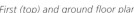

First (top) and ground floor plans

Renovation and partial storey addition to an old coach house in Berlin's Treptow district. An open area was created on the ground floor with kitchen and dining area, while bedroom and study are partitioned off by sliding doors. The living room is situated in the roof addition, which is surrounded by a large roof terrace on three sides. The basement offers storage space. A new spiral stair connects all three floors. The rooms are characterised by the merger of historic masonry and new, white installations. Walls and ceilings were cleaned and plastered with lime slurry. The floor consists of a pigmented heating screed.

Sliding doors in front of bedroom and study (above), kitchen und spiral stair (below)

Haus Stein

| Bauernstrasse 10 | GFA 240 m² | **JAN RÖSLER ARCHITEKTEN** | Client: private |
| 39365 Druxberge | GV 610 m³ | www.janroesler.de | |

Exterior view

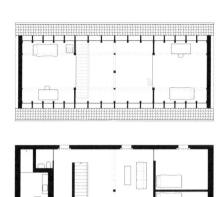

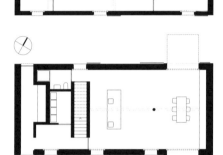

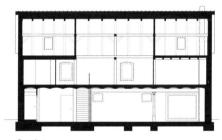

Ground, first and gallery floor plans

Section

Conversion of a barn to a holiday house in the Magdeburg Börde region. The building interior was reorganised. A wide area with kitchen, dining area, stove and two outdoor terraces was created on the ground floor. Stairs lead up to a living hall on the upper floor that reaches up to the ridge. The bedrooms and bathroom area are placed at the gable ends. The galleries above these enclosed rooms are open to the hall. The external appearance of the barn has been preserved: its use as a holiday house only becomes evident when the wooden doors and shutters are opened. The owners performed most of the conversion work. First and foremost, sustainable construction materials, such as clay, wood, flax or recycled stones, were used. Annual energy consumption was reduced to 59 kWh/m², thanks to internal soft wood fibre, flat insulation in the roof and insulated glazing.

Living hall with gallery (above), dining area and fireplace on the ground floor (below)

Holiday House in Lühsdorf

| Dorfstrasse 2a | GFA 170 m² | **Eva Mayer-Laipple** | | Client: private |
| 14929 Lühsdorf | GV 440 m³ | www.evamayerlaipple.de | | |

View from the southeast

Upper floor

New construction of a holiday house in a village south of Berlin. The form of the house replicates a barn. Roof and the façade are clad with untreated larch boards. Inside, white walls and robust materials such as brick, wood and concrete determine the ambience. Kitchen, living and dining area, bathroom and bedroom are located on the ground floor. The finished attic storey provides space for the children, a guest room and second bathroom. Sauna and wood storage are housed in a flat-roofed ancillary building. The ground floor and gable walls were built in solid construction. The attic storey is framed in wood. A gas condensing boiler ensures basic heating for the rooms, using underfloor heating on the ground floor. A wood-burning stove provides heat in the living area.

Lounge (above), dining area and kitchen (below)

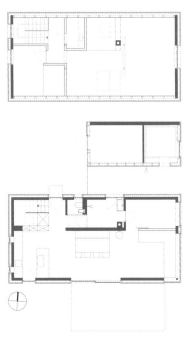

Upper (top) und ground floor plans

The Maple Leaf revisited

Are postwar buildings better protected than they were sixteen years ago?

*Haus des Lehrers on Alexanderplatz (left),
Ahornblatt restaurant in 1989 (above)*

The summer of 2000 was a dark time for listed buildings in Berlin. The Ahornblatt, or Maple Leaf, a striking structure with a leaf-shaped roof built on the Fischerinsel as a canteen, was demolished. This happened despite protests from architects, a conference resolution by the Chamber of Architects, and a barrage of newspaper articles. Responsibility for its destruction lay not only with the developer, which had acquired the site with planning permission for a high-density development, nor his architect, whose original design also included two slender towers beside the restaurant. In the end this proposal did not fit in with the plans of the city's development administration, and of senate construction director Hans Stimmann. Moreover, there was little public support for the preservation of the restaurant, designed by Ulrich Müther in the early 1970s. "East Berliners are surprisingly passionless about the future of the Ahornblatt," architectural journalist Peter Rumpf wrote at the time.

Even today, many Berliners are not only passionless about postwar Modernist architecture, but rather hostile towards it, despite the efforts of the profession itself, and of university researchers who enthuse about the merits of this era. Meanwhile, a new generation, born after these buildings were constructed, is beginning to regard them with a growing affection. Between 2003 and 2006, architects and artists passionately campaigned for a series of individual buildings that were in danger of being torn down. There was the *ZwischenPalastNutzung* initiative for the Palast der Republik; there was the *atelier für alles* group who tried to save the distinctive aluminium façade of the department store on Alexanderplatz by auctioning off some of its honeycomb-shaped elements; and there were Oliver Elser and Andreas Muhs whose website, *restmodern.de*, provided a showcase for lesser-known examples of postwar architecture.

The fiftieth birthday of Interbau, the 1957 International Building Exhibition, occurred in 2007. The event was marked by a series of publications and exhibitions, such as *Denkmal!Moderne*, organised by the Schinkel-Zentrum at Berlin Technical University and the Arbeitsgemeinschaft Gefährdete Nachkriegsmoderne. And four organisations representing people who lived and worked in postwar buildings merged to form *Schaustelle Nachkriegsmoderne*, whose goal was to give greater prominence to buildings of that era. Finally, 2013 saw the publication of a groundbreaking work: Adrian von Buttlar, Kerstin Wittmann-Englert and Gabi Dolff-Bonekämper catalogued 262 buildings in *Architekturführer Berlin 1949–1979 – Baukunst der Nachkriegsmoderne*. "Our heritage is widely threatened by demolition and defacement," they wrote.

Could the Ahornblatt have been demolished today? "Attitudes towards postwar modern architecture have improved significantly since 2000," says Bernhard Kohlenbach of the Landesdenkmalamt, the Berlin listing department. He has laboriously extracted from his organisation's database all eighty or so listed commercial buildings from the period. These are mostly shops, offices and government buildings, but also include factories, cinemas, hotels, and specialist structures such as the Fernsehturm. Unlike cultural and educational buildings, they are often owned by companies and thus subject

to specific financial constraints. Listing commercial buildings is therefore dependent on public and political will, and on owners who regard the listing of their property as an asset and an opportunity rather than a liability.

Getting buildings listed is only the first step towards recognition: how they are saved is much more important than whether they are. Many redevelopment projects have shown that there is a fine line between preservation, sensitive modernisation, and desecration. Probably the biggest challenge is preserving as much as possible of the original structures and adapting them to meet climate protection and energy efficiency targets, but many owners are reluctant to pay for this, and façades are losing the fine detail that was often the reason for their being listed in the first place.

There are some honourable exceptions, like the 2004 renovation of the Kiepert-Haus on Hardenbergstrasse, whose old steel-framed composite windows were restored by Winkens Architekten. And in 2007, Platena Jagusch Architekten renovated the altered façade of the Osram-Haus on Ernst-Reuter-Platz using red balustrades based on the originals. Another survivor was the elegant exterior of the George C. Marshall-Haus on Messedamm, although in 2008 Modersohn & Freiesleben Architekten replaced the steel and glass façade with a thermally isolated steel and aluminium structure to save energy.

Perhaps the most prominent renovation in recent times is the Bikini-Haus on Breitscheidplatz, reopened as a concept mall in 2014 in what the operators called a "judicious revitalisation".

But amid all the enthusiasm over the renaissance of the City West district, there has been little discussion of whether the reconstruction represents a success for listed building preservation. It destroyed the distinctive stairwells on the back of the structure, built over the courtyard, added another storey on top, reduced the depth of the colonnade, and replaced the old zoo-facing façade with a new version, and the Breitscheidplatz façade with an imitation of the old one.

When you consider how many buildings have been knocked down, it is easy to look at the Bikini-Haus and say it could have been worse. But if you regard it as an integral part of Breitscheidplatz, a symbol of the US-funded rebuilding of the western sector, its importance extends well beyond the boundaries of Berlin. The building's current appearance is at least a partial success for the cause of preservation. After acquiring the building in 2002 the developer, Bayerische Hausbau, took nearly ten years to come up with a plan for the site, and the listing authorities negotiated a series of back-room compromises. As for the neighbouring Schimmelpfeng-Haus, the senate was clearly in no mood for compromise, and the building was reduced to a heap of rubble in 2009. As with the Ahornblatt, the demolition was the result of the inner city development plan, which provided for two high-rise buildings on this site.

Breitscheidplatz's equivalent in East Berlin, Alexanderplatz, has changed a lot since 2000. The campaign to save the aluminium façade of the former Centrum department store was unsuccessful, and it was replaced by sandstone slabs, but the Haus

Haus des Reisens (left) and
Haus des Berliner Verlages (right) on Alexanderplatz,
Bikini-Haus on Breitscheidplatz (below)

des Lehrers and Kongresshalle have been renovated in accordance with listing requirements. In July 2015, three more postwar structures were added to the list: the world clock, the Haus des Reisens and the Haus des Berliner Verlages. The senate pointed out that this completed the listing of East German architecture around Alexanderplatz. A review was begun in 2015 of whether the existing development plans and contracts are compatible with the buildings' new listed status, because Hans Kollhoff's winning competition entry from over twenty years ago, which involved surrounding Alexanderplatz with high-rise buildings, was still valid. If we're not careful, the postwar Modernist buildings on Alexanderplatz might suffer the same fate as those on Breitscheidplatz. As resources grow scarcer, any renovation has to be better than demolition and new construction, and we need good examples to persuade the developers. The responsibility lies with listing specialists in government departments and universities, architects, planners, engineers, owners, politicians offering subsidy programmes, and environmental campaigners.

But Berlin's postwar Modernist architecture is faring better than it was in 2000. A 2014 conference in Weimar on the listing of postwar Modernist buildings in eastern Germany heard that many other German cities are eyeing Berlin with envy. Berlin has a committed network of activists in academia, conservation, architecture and other disciplines, and the combative opposition to the wholesale urban renewal of the 1970s has clearly survived, albeit in a different form. Even the politicians now in

charge seem to have grasped the importance of postwar Modernism: after years of infighting, the senate recently announced that the giant ICC conference centre, long scheduled for demolition, was to be listed.

Soho House Berlin

Torstrasse 1	GFA (new building)	300 m²	**gbp Architekten**	Client: Cresco Capital
10119 Berlin	GFA (existing structure)	15,700 m²	www.gbp-architekten.de	
	GV (new building)	3,000 m³		
	GV (existing structure)	57,300 m³		

Suite

Conversion of a listed building into a private member club for creative people from the worlds of media, design, film, music and fashion. The building was opened in 1929 as a department store. After World War II, it was used by the Socialist Unity Party. The study of East Germany's former president, Wilhelm Pieck, has survived from that period. Today, 65 hotel rooms, 24 serviced apartments, lofts and suites, several bars, a cinema, spa, gym, restaurant, event rooms and a roof terrace with pool are distributed throughout 10 storeys. The building was refurbished in accordance with conservation guidelines and the risalto façade was rebuilt. However, several building sections had to be completely renewed. A new spiral stair connects the basement, ground and first floors. The renovation included analysis and elimination of hazardous materials such as PCBs, tar products and asbestos.

View from the street

Lobby (above), bar and new spiral stair (below)

AZIMUT St. Petersburg

Lermontovsky Prospekt 43/1
190103 St. Petersburg
(Russia)

GFA 13,000 m²

BRUZKUS BATEK
www.bruzkusbatek.com

Client: Azimut Hotels Company

Sky bar

Conference area

Redesign of a hotel's interiors. The three-star-plus category establishment occupies an 18-storey high-rise built in 1967. The project is part of an ongoing development of a new corporate design for the hotel chain initiated in 2011. This design is refined and solidified with each new project. Many items such as side tables, sofas and chairs were specially designed for the hotel chain. In addition to the rooms and halls, BRUZKUS BATEK also designed the lobby and its restaurant, two conference areas containing a total of ten rooms and the sky bar.

Lobby (above), room, hall and restaurant (below)

Löwen-Apotheke

| Hauptmarkt 6 | GFA 270 m² | **Glahn Architekten** | Clients: |
| 54290 Trier | GV 1,000 m³ | www.glahn architekten de | Dr Claus and Dr Elisabeth Schmiz |

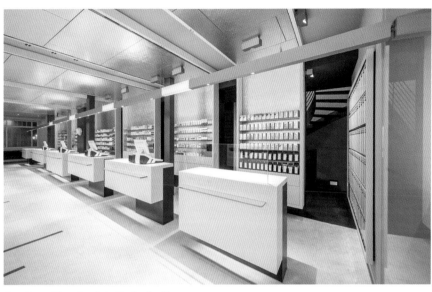

Counters with a view into the back office

The pharmacy's history on display

Redesign and furnishing of a pharmacy. The pharmacy was mentioned in a document as early as 1241 and is considered the oldest in Germany. It is now located in an architectural monument built in 1649. All interior walls were removed in the conversion. The long, funnel-shaped retail space extends through the entire depth of the building. The glazed dispensary is situated at the narrow end with a view of a tree of life (gingko) in the redesigned atrium. A back-office area (with office and medicine dispenser on the upper floor) parallels the retail space. Clear lines and natural materials define the ambience. For example, ceiling and rear wall panels in gold leaf enhance the interior, while providing a reminder of old brass mortars. The original colours of a 1690 Cologne plaster ceiling were exposed in the entrance area.

Retail space with plaster ceiling from 1649

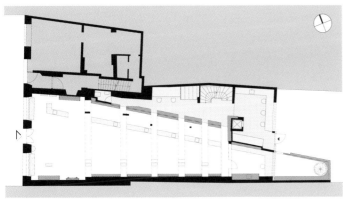

Floor plan

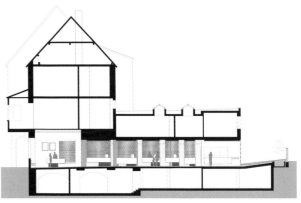

Section

Barceló Centre

Calle de Barceló, 6
28004 Madrid
(Spain)

GFA 43,050 m²
GV   152,800 m³
Usable open space 30,300 m²

Nieto Sobejano Arquitectos
www.nietosobejano.de

Client: Municipality of Madrid

View from the north

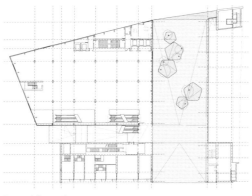

Ground floor plan

Site plan

New building complex in a densely-built quarter of Madrid. The individual structures form an urban puzzle. A four-storey market hall and parking garage at the southeast corner provide the prelude. An internal gallery street separates the sports centre on its northwest flank. A narrow structure for its first five floors, the sports centre expands at the sixth floor and projects, like a pavilion, far over the terrace on the hall roof. At the western boundary, a new library building closes the playground of a school, completing the block formed by its buildings. A long city plaza emerged between the library and hall complex. During the construction period, the *Mercado Municipal* was housed in a nearby, specially-built temporary structure.

Overall view (above), sports centre over the market hall (below)

BAIC Headquarters Beijing Automotive R&D Centre

99 Shuang He Da Jie
101300 Beijing
(China)

GFA 155,000 m²
GV 713,000 m³

GKK+Architekten Ges. von Architekten mbH
Prof. Swantje Kühn, Oliver Kühn
www.gkk-architekten.de

Client: BAIC Beijing
Automotive Industry Holding Company

Exterior view

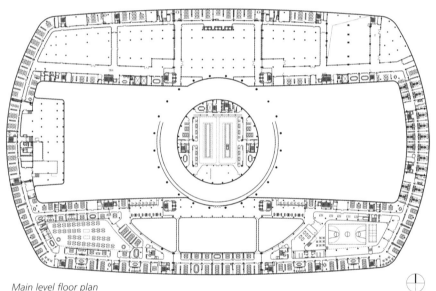

Main level floor plan

Catwalk at the central circular structure

New headquarters building with development centre for the largest automotive industry supplier in China. The complex is located in the Shunyi borough at Beijing's new airport. Its form recreates a car body. Its façade is clad in metal. The centre contains office spaces, training and conference areas, laboratories, design studios and workshops for 2,700 people plus a hotel. The main entrance is at the side. Conference and restaurant areas flank the three-storey entrance hall. A circular structure in the middle accommodates the design studios, model-building workshops and exhibition areas. A curved catwalk connects it to the offices at the perimeter.

Entrance hall (above), access road (below)

ERBE Lounge

Waldhörnlestrasse 17
72072 Tübingen

GFA 105 m²
GV 315 m³

claim Skaba Flothmann
Planungsgesellschaft GbR
www.claimspace.de

Client: ERBE Elektromedizin GmbH

Exhibition in the outer corridor

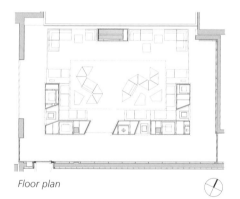

Floor plan

Interior design for a medical technology company. The lounge links the old and new buildings; a transitional space between staircases and foyer. Exhibits and milestones presented in graphic and media formats stage the 150 years of company history as a succession of innovations. Floor-to-ceiling displays along the outer corridor frame the actual lounge. Its casually grouped seating elements can be rearranged as required. Thus, the exhibition forms the framework for a place of interaction that communicates company values and the tradition of collaboration to guests and staff. The project was carried out in collaboration with Büro Achter April, Architektur Schmitt Dannien Hofmann Partnergesellschaft (overall measures), maierlighting (lighting) and conservator Anne Bührer.

Lounge

Workshop Building

Wollankstrasse 134
13187 Berlin

GFA (new building)　140 m²
GFA (existing structure) 35 m²
GV (new building)　465 m³
GV (existing structure) 115 m³

Architekturbüro Schmid
www.arch-schmid.de

Client: private

View from the courtyard

Site plan

Modernisation of a former workshop building in the courtyard of a listed house once situated on the village green. The half-timbered building from around 1900 was in desolate condition and infested with dry rot. A new timber building takes up its volume and includes the old masonry. The new building permits commercial and residential use. White enamelled wood, clay and felt are the defining materials in the interior design, each with a clear function. Felt curtains allow flexible division of space. Clay rendering on the masonry improves the interior climate, and wood as the primary construction material makes it possible to achieve insulation that complies with the passive house standard by simple means. Reeds in a pool in front of the floor-length window façade on the ground floor provide the workspaces with some distance from the events in the courtyard.

Upper floor interior (above) and ground floor with stairs (below)

ESA_

Schlüterstrasse 73	GFA (new building)	230 m²	**wiewiorra hopp schwark architekten**	Client: private
10625 Berlin	GFA (existing structure)	410 m²	www.whs-architekten.de	
	GV (new building)	795 m³		
	GV (existing structure)	1,425 m³		

View from the courtyard

Ground floor plan

Partial conversion and expansion of a 1966 residential and commercial building
in Berlin's Charlottenburg district. As a first step in the physical modernisation of the
building, the ground floor was modified and a two-storey extension was added on the
courtyard side. In the process, the courtyard access, which previously split the areas on
the ground floor into two inefficient units, was moved to one side. At the same time,
this created space for a new foyer in front of the central staircase. A law office occupies
the ground and first floor spaces enlarged by the extension. A separate stairway connects the two floors. It is part of a new structure enclosing the staircase. This structure
also incorporates a kitchenette, wardrobe and storage room.

Courtyard access with main entrance (above), integrated stairway to the first floor (below)

Ritterhof

Ritterstrasse 11
10969 Berlin

GFA 17,200 m²
GV 57,175 m³

WAF Architekten
www.waf-architekten.de

Client: Francap S.A.R.L.

Office loft

View from the street

Site plan

Restoration and modernisation of a listed 1906 commercial building in Berlin's Kreuzberg district. 11,000 square metres of office lofts for an online portal were created on six floors. Together with the black and white colour scheme and mastic asphalt floors with industrial coating, the preserved solid floors and brick walls emphasise the original, industrial character. Glass walls partition off the few individual offices and conference rooms, thus preserving the visual openness of the lofts. Exposed columns, unconcealed building services and white woodwool slabs that improve acoustics also contribute to the industrial ambience. On the ground floor, an in-house day care facility, canteen and café complement the building use. The façade was renovated around 1990 and remained unaltered. Only a few metal doors were removed and the courtyard access from the street was redesigned.

Office loft (above), staircase with old preserved and new access doors (below)

3
AUFGANG 2
← A B →

Greifswalder Strasse 212

Greifswalder	GFA (new building)	3,800 m²
Strasse 212	GFA (existing structure)	5,600 m²
10405 Berlin	GV (new building)	15,575 m³
	GV (existing structure)	22,950 m³

Klaus Schlosser Architekten BDA
www.klausschlosserarchitekten.com

Client: Prime Management
GmbH & Co. KG

Commercial floor

Conversion and completion of a commercial complex in the Prenzlauer Berg district. The inventory dates back to the end of the 19th century, the 1920s and the 1960s. The older structures (around the front courtyard) were renovated in 2008. Now, the industrial construction from the post-war period that forms the second courtyard has been thoroughly rehabilitated and modernised. A long, two-storey building that completes the courtyard development, an underground garage and a staircase for the entire complex are newly built. Inclined footbridges and ramp stairs connect storeys of differing heights within the structures. The *Shed* relief tile, with a glaze matched to the colour of the late 19th century elevations, was specially developed for the façades.

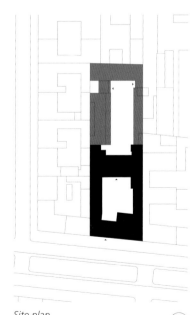

Site plan

Courtyard with renovated old buildings and new, elongated building (above), footbridge and main entrance (below)

Fresh Monument Protection

12205 Berlin   GFA 450 m²
                   GV   2,320 m³

Maedebach & Redeleit Architekten
www.maedebach-redeleit.de

Corridor

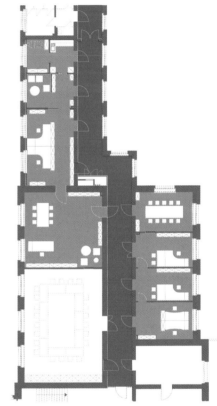

Floor plan

Conversion and renovation of an institute head office. The reception, offices and meeting rooms are located in a listed, 1903 clinker brick building. Later installations were removed from every room. Surfaces and special building elements such as vaulted ceilings or period doors and double casement windows were exposed and restored. Contemporary furnishings and a modern illumination system emphasise the institute's progressive orientation. New building services (including air-conditioning) were integrated without compromising the historical building substance.

Secretariat (above), presidential office and office (below)

Königs Wusterhausen Town Hall

Schlossstrasse 4
15711 Königs Wusterhausen

GFA 2,375 m²
GV 8,900 m³

Numrich Albrecht Klumpp
Gesellschaft von Architekten mbH
www.nak-architekten.de

Client: City of Königs Wusterhausen

Stairway outside the council chamber

Foyer and staircase

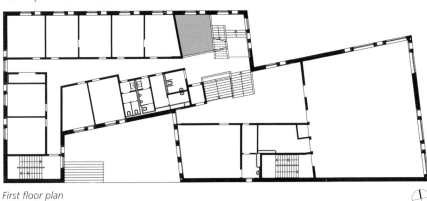

First floor plan

New building for the public and formal areas of the town administration. The building faces the castle and is connected by a corridor to the adjacent old town hall, which still accommodates offices. Since this link is glazed, the visual axis between the castle and the historical Amtsgarten is maintained. The split levels of the new building contain the council chamber, mayor's office, wedding room and citizens' services. The floor plan of the double-gable building is almost S-shaped. A recess in the front portion of the building creates an entrance plaza. A second recess at the rear forms a terrace in front of the registry office. The building's energy consumption is 25 percent below the requirements of German law.

View from Schlossstrasse (above), council chamber (below)

Federal Ministry of Education and Research

Kapelle-Ufer 1
10117 Berlin

GFA 58,000 m²
GV 213,000 m³

Heinle, Wischer und Partner
www.heinlewischerpartner.de

Client: Institute for Federal Real Estate

Connecting footbridge next to the city railway

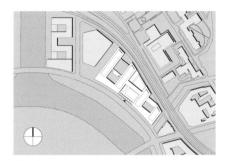

Site plan

View from the River Spree

New Berlin headquarters building. The six-storey complex is situated near the central station at a bend in the River Spree. Two office wings with U-shaped floor plans are united by a recessed link. This results in a court that is open to the river and contains the main entrance. Bands of natural stone and vertical solar and glass elements between floor-to-ceiling windows define the façade. The interior climate of the offices can be individually controlled. The building achieves key aspects of sustainable construction: low energy consumption, innovative technical systems, low-pollution materials and accessibility. For this it received gold certification in accordance with the Sustainable Construction for Federal Buildings (BNB) evaluation system. The energy consumed by the complex is mainly produced on-site with fuel cells, combined heat and power plant and photovoltaic panels.

View from the street (above), foyer and conference level (below)

Fast-lane modernity

The forgotten qualities of a post-war traffic infrastructure project

*Steglitz Junction in 2015 (left),
Halensee Interchange in 1960 (above)*

Berlin's *Stadtautobahn* has once again become a construction site with the announcement of a number of major projects. The Rudolf Wissell Bridge is to be completely replaced and the AVUS Interchange, currently known as the Funkturm 3-Way Interchange, will be modernised. In light of these significant interventions, it seems timely to take a closer to look at this now 60-year-old work of transport infrastructure: a motorway that, in addition to its primary role as a transportation route, offers users a particular perspective on the city. This aspect was explored by Wim Wenders in his 1987 film *Wings of Desire*, documenting the flow of traffic, and the motorway's structural caesuras and fractures. Wenders intuitively recognised the cinematic qualities of this roadway, which, with its gently curving gradient and uniform flow, creates an aesthetic experience of memorable transience.

Between 1956 and 1964, the most important sections along the route between Halenseestrasse and Jakob-Kaiser-Platz were completed – receiving both considerable attention and widespread public approval. When in 1965/66 the German Federal Post Office Berlin published a series of stamps showcasing 12 notable buildings in West Berlin under the title *The New Berlin*, it was only natural that the *Stadtautobahn* was included in this collection alongside the Philharmonie, the Europa-Center, and the Deutsche Oper. The designers chose the Halensee Interchange, completed in 1957, to represent the motorway, presenting an iconic ensemble of motorway and cityscape that was to appear on thousands of postcards together with the AVUS Interchange and became a synonym of a modern Berlin.

With the sweeping line of the elongated ramps forming a basket handle curve as they embrace the tunnel entrance, and the elegant, flowing curvature of the graded lane separation, the Halensee Interchange presents a dynamic picture. The composition of the interchange, together with Felix Hinssen's high-rise apartment block (1955–1958) and the sweeping lines of the roading on Rathenauplatz, makes for a rhythmic, staggered urban ensemble that reflects the ideal of an open, green and mobile city. Even today, this composition underscores the role of the *Stadtautobahn* within a wider radical makeover which sought to position the isolated city-state of Berlin as a modern metropolis and an appealing window onto the western world.

All of the interchanges and on- and off-ramps built in these early phases were notable for their elaborate designs. The Schmargendorf Flyover, constructed from 1959 to 1960, is notable not only for the generous and varied curvature of the roading. The parabolic form of the hollow box girders supporting the exit for Steglitz also presents an emphatically plastic view from below. The result – viewed together with Wilmersdorf power plant (built 1973–1977) – is an impressive vision of the modern metropolis that presents itself to the viewer in motion. Numerous perspective drawings preserved from the planning process make it clear that the *Stadtautobahn* was from the very outset conceived not simply as a transportation solution but as an aesthetic experience as well. These include various large-format charcoal drawings by Werner Düttmann, which he prepared in 1958 in his role as Senate Building Inspector. Düttmann was responsible for the planning of numerous civil engineering works in connection with the *Stadtautobahn* – including the design of the Ost-

preussenbrücke (1958 to 1960) with its striking V-shape supports. One year later the flowing arc of the Rudolf Wissell Bridge – spanning close to one kilometre in length – was officially opened. The slender, pre-stressed concrete structure rests on just 12 H-shaped double supports and – with its double curvature built in the balanced cantilever method – is not only a masterpiece of engineering, but also a particularly elegant work of transportation infrastructure. The bridge's smooth, gliding motion in a wide arc over the landscape made it possible for motorists to experience the ancient glacial valley that cuts through Berlin.

The most elaborate interchange built in this context connects the *Stadtautobahn* to the AVUS, probably the oldest metropolitan motorway in Europe. Aerial photographs from the early 1960s reveal a landscape of neatly trimmed lawns and lightly planted groves between the roadways: a clean design that evokes associations with landscaped gardens and enables passers-by and motorists to experience the interlacing graded lanes from a range of perspectives. According to the brief from 1962, the planners undertook to create with the AVUS Interchange a unified entity that combined roading, built structures and green spaces. This achievement is perhaps best viewed from the observation deck

of the nearby Berlin Radio Tower. Viewed from the observation deck, it is clear that the design was inspired by the Pretzel interchange on the New York Grand Central Parkway, a work that was lauded by Sigfried Giedion in his 1941 book *Space, Time and Architecture* as the epitome of modernity.

Given the tremendous advances in motorisation seen in the USA, American roads and road infrastructure were considered to be the *non plus ultra* – and were studied closely by the planners involved in the development of the *Stadtautobahn* in several research trips to the USA undertaken in the years from 1953 to 1957. The elaborate gradient design implemented here also suggest that planners drew on previous experiences in landscape sensitive motorway design – as developed in Germany in the 1930s in an aesthetic sensibility which prized the even flow of traffic. The result was a cinematic choreography of the automotive gaze as the motorist progresses through the metropolitan landscape. Another notable feature of West Berlin's *Stadtautobahn* was the integration – planned from the outset – of express bus lines with stops located along the roadway itself. This was presumably inspired by the successful implementation of similar infrastructure in Detroit, where 64 bus lines had serviced the metropolitan free-

Motorway bridges at Steglitz Junction (left),
Kurfürstendamm/Halensee motorway exit viewed from
the Funkturm (right), BAB 100 at Kaiserdamm (below)

ways since the mid-1950s. In Berlin, where many of the bus stops were accessible by escalator, a variety of idiosyncratic architectural designs were implemented. Many of these were successively dismantled after regular bus services along the route ceased in 1993, including the double stairway on Jakob-Kaiser-Platz with its bright orange ceramic shell. A classically Modernist pavilion built at the Witzleben bus stop in 1959 is now occupied by a snack bar. The bus station buildings on Bundesplatz differ significantly in terms of their design, and fill a narrow gap between the roadway and the adjacent buildings. The station is a tightly structured ensemble in raw concrete with dense lines of horizontal window slits that evoke associations with the dynamic façades of Erich Mendelsohn. Inside, the stations sport the vibrantly coloured ceramic iconography of public transport that ensures each station bears a distinctive visual identity and eases navigation.

A ride on the sections of motorway built between 1956 and 1976 presents a series of diverging visions of the future. The generous use of space and landscaped layout of the sections built initially presented motorists with a dynamic and fundamentally new experience of the city. From the mid-1960s onward, more unusual and highly technical architectures were explicitly adapted to the motorway as a space of aesthetic experience. Notable examples of this practice include the transportation *Gesamtkunstwerk* that is Tegel Airport (1965–1975); the ICC with its stunning architectural design and skilful integration within the interweaving traffic lanes; the *Bierpinsel* restaurant tower in Steglitz; and the first ever large-scale residential complex built above a motorway on Schlangenbader Strasse.

This spectacular coupling of a motorway and residential highrise building exemplifies the paradigm change of the 1970s. Until then inner-city expressways had figured as aesthetic and programmatic stages for the representation of the modern metropolis – in West Berlin, as elsewhere. But the advent of mass motorisation and the oil crisis transformed the *Stadtautobahn* – once a prestige project – into an object of functional infra-

structure that was increasingly viewed as a foreign body rather than a gateway to the city. Since then the motorway has been upgraded with various technical and structural measures in an attempt to mitigate its negative impact on the city.

Any contemporary appraisal of these massive and in many cases problematic works must embrace a nuanced perspective that considers their architectural and cultural-historical qualities. After all, who can tell whether the bus stops along the motorway might not return to service as new trends in mobility gain traction, or whether the motorway's visual qualities might not again find popular appeal? What is quite evident, however, is that aesthetic considerations most certainly played a role in the planning processes. As late as 1973 Elmar Oehm noted in his standard work on metropolitan motorways: "Motorways should not be simply routes for the collection and distribution of traffic, they should be imposing works of civil engineering within our cities and expressions of our times and mindset."

P1 Multi-storey Car Park at Hamburg Airport

Flughafenstrasse 1–3
22335 Hamburg

GFA 76,050 m²
GV 221,000 m³

Riegler Riewe Architekten
www.rieglerriewe.de

Client: Flughafen Hamburg GmbH

Façade at the entrance

Site plan

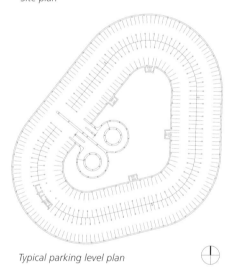

Typical parking level plan

New construction of a multi-storey car park with almost 2,800 spaces as the result of a competition in 2011. The five-storey building with six parking levels was built on an irregular area, known as the *little almond*, in the network of access and exit roads from the airport. The parking spaces are arranged in two double rows along the sides of a triangle with rounded corners. The spiral entrance and exit ramps form a double tower in the wide interior courtyard. The courtyard provides daylight and ample ventilation and makes orientation easier. Horizontal precast reinforced concrete lamellas encompass the exterior façade of the ringed structure. Complementing the row of circular buildings standing at the approach to the airport, it forms a striking landmark, clearly identifiable from every surrounding roadway.

View from the street (above), courtyard (below)

'Buggy Bin' Pram Shelter

Fischerinsel 3	GFA 20 m²	**LEGEER ARCHITEKTEN**	Client: Kreativhaus e.V.
10179 Berlin	GV 52 m³	www.legeer.de	

Internal view

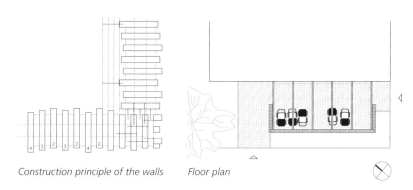

Construction principle of the walls   *Floor plan*

New construction of a weather-proof shelter for up to 13 buggies. This small structure was erected on the grounds of Kreativhaus e.V. on Berlin's Fischerinsel. Its walls consist of boards varnished in two clear tones of green and blue. Their staggered assembly adds relief to the walls. The boards are spaced apart at eye level. These gaps align into a kind of continuous window that allows a view from the inside. The transparent roof consists of multi-skin sheets. The same boards are used in its substructure as for the walls. All of the elements can be reused after deconstruction. Built as a social project, the Buggy Bin was constructed almost exclusively by participants in re-integration measures.

Exterior view by day (above) and night (below)

Simone Hübener

Scouting locations

Event halls strive to be adaptable, profitable and iconic

*Mehr! Theatre in Hamburg (left),
Mercedes-Benz Arena in Berlin (above)*

In the 1990s, the Americanisation of the cultural life in Germany gained momentum: the public sector backed off from funding projects, while international business stepped in with sponsorship funds, mostly from the private sector. At the same time, event halls grew in capacity. The events themselves became gigantic undertakings, the sheer number of spectators being the best way to break even at the end of the year. This dynamic has influenced the architecture of arenas and concert halls.

One of the largest European facilities of this type is the former 17,000-seat O_2 World arena in Berlin, now known as the Mercedes-Benz Arena since 2015. Securing the naming rights to the arena was one of the best things that could have happened to the global automotive corporation – after all, its German sales headquarters are only 100 metres from the arena. Both the arena and the spacious plaza just in front of the building, now also named after the car brand, have given Mercedes-Benz a very high profile in the Friedrichshain-Kreuzberg borough of Berlin.

Outside, the sponsor name change is readily apparent. Gone is the distinctive blue colour of mobile phone provider O_2, replaced by the black and dark grey of Mercedes-Benz corporate design. The company names were also switched out. However, what Mercedes-Benz describes in a press release as its "commitment to Berlin" goes beyond simply dismantling the old logo and putting up its own. The company is making every effort – at times more subtly, at others more overtly – to draw attention to the brand. This major investment is also meant to improve the arena's architecture and atmosphere. A Mercedes star nearly 50 feet tall has been painted on the roof to make sure the building is visible from the air. (Hello Google Maps!) The interior looks more elegant than it did during the O_2 era. Black, dark grey and silver set the tone, just as they do in the brand's dealerships, with state-of-the art technology as part of the makeover. Warmer LED downlights replace the former fluorescent light tubes. High-resolution LCD monitors now stand in place of a pixelated LED wall. Depending on the event and audience, various car models are displayed outdoors, thus completing the fusion of arena and sponsor.

In Baku, the capital of Azerbaijan, the Baku Crystal Hall is the flagship building of a government rather than a company. This indisputably unique project was constructed for the 2012 Eurovision Song Contest. From planning to inauguration, building the hall only took one year. The normal estimate for a project of this kind is four years. It was only possible to complete it in such a short time because the president of Azerbaijan would speed up the issuing of building permits whenever necessary. He was also intent on seizing the opportunity to present his country to the world – no matter what the cost. The project owed its success to the close collaboration and solid foundation of trust between the companies involved in the project – notably the Alpine construction company, the Berlin office of gmp – Architekten von Gerkan, Marg und Partner, and Nussli, a specialist in temporary event structures. The design and construction team alone comprised 111 people (not including employees of subcontractors). At peak times, some 1,500 individuals worked on the construction site.

To meet the tight deadlines, planners divided the building into three sections: the hall itself, with supporting structure, grandstands, grandstand roof and thermal façade; the interior roof, which can be retracted for open-air events such as football games or to draw out smoke in the event of fire; and the membrane façade system and its steelwork. This division of labour allowed planning, construction and on-site assembly to happen simultaneously. The architectural highlight of the 128.5 x 90.5-metre hall is its membrane façade system, comprising 180 panels that wrap around the entire building. These are equipped with 83,000 LEDs that combine to create 9,000 points of light, a work by the Berlin lighting design firm Lichtvision. This membrane makes the building visible at night and from afar, gives it an ever-changing appearance and produces effective images for media use. Such issues were all very important to the building owner. The government in Baku did not want to miss out on the opportunity for self-promotion in what promised to be a major media event for the country.

Even as major event facilities are being built, the industry is witnessing another trend: smaller cultural venues in older buildings, often listed as historic landmarks, and more impressive and distinctive in their architecture and atmosphere. Sponsorship is either non-existent or handled in a much more discreet manner. Perhaps the first hall of this type was the Arena Berlin in the Treptow district, which was up and running as early as 1995. The building was designed as a bus depot by architect Franz

Ahrens in the 1920s. Its 70-metre span made it the largest self-supporting hall in Europe at the time. The building is an example of Expressionist architecture in Berlin and now figures on the city's list of historic monuments.

Former Arena Berlin owner Falk Walter transformed this hall into a trendy, prominent venue without any public or private financial support. Its eclectic programme offers theatre presentations, concerts, company events, and recently trade fairs. Strong demand for the location resulted in several capacity expansions – from 6,000 people to 9,000 and now 10,000. Fire safety was also improved during a 2014 renovation. Until then, trade fairs were only allowed with special permits as they in-

Simone Hübener

*Baku Crystal Hall during a light show by Licht & Söhne (left),
Mehr! Theatre in the Hamburg wholesale market hall (below),
Arena Berlin (lower left)*

volve a higher fire load. Wilk Salins Architekten focused entirely on the existing structure and used a colour scheme and materials that managed to preserve the building's sense of space. The project is an example of how vision, courage and expertise can be put to work to make the most of an existing building.

A similar example is Hamburg's Mehr! Theatre, which opened in March 2015 with a concert by the London Symphony Orchestra. This new theatre was created inside the Hamburg wholesale food market, a three-section hall designed by Bernhard Hermkes and constructed in Hamburg's Hammerbrook district between 1958 and 1962. The listed building is an important example of experimental prestressed concrete construction and is still used as a market hall. Some 1.5 million tons of fruit, vegetables and flowers are bought and sold here daily. The new theatre occupies 4,000 square metres – 10 percent of the hall's floor space. F101 Architekten from Berlin proceeded with extreme caution and merely inserted all of the new theatre structures into the hall. The insert can be dismantled as needed without causing any damage to the prominent roof construction. This alternative cultural use is practical. Market operations are restricted to the early morning hours; in the evening, the theatre throws open its doors. The project also helped the theatre operators, who probably could have never afforded the cost of a new building.

The design highlight of Mehr! Theatre is the way in which the rooms form one continuous space. Only the cloakroom and a small waiting area are separated from the rest of the theatre, whereas the foyer and bar area merge with the theatre hall. The space is also suitable for concerts, fairs and corporate events. Understated grey and black tones make up the colour scheme. Only a few fluorescent lights emit colours. Sponsors' names are displayed only on the outside, a feature deliberately stipulated by the architecture firm in collaboration with the entire team. Two versions of 4.5-metre-high letters are intended to display the name of the sponsoring company on the vast premises, a standing set and one lying on the ground. The letters lying on the ground also double as seating. This idea of the architects is intelligent in more than one respect: it distances the sponsorship physically from the building, respecting the building's status as a protected historical monument. What is more, this distance creates a plaza in front of the theatre entrance. Such positioning ultimately benefits sponsors, since small illuminated letters on the façade would be completely lost in the huge dimensions of the complex.

Dentists in the Imperial Hall

Kurfürsten-
damm 193d
10707 Berlin

GFA (new building) 36 m²
GFA (existing structure) 220 m²
GV (new building) 130 m³
GV (existing structure) 950 m³

TREILING architekten
www.treiling.com

Client: Andreas Bothe

Stairway to the gallery

*Gallery (top) and
entrance level floor plans*

Conversion of half a ballroom into a dental practice. The listed Haus Cumberland
on the Kurfürstendamm opened as a boarding house in 1912. Today, following restoration and conversion, it serves as a residential and commercial property. The ballroom was
brutally subdivided after World War II. Its glorious decor only remained preserved in this
half. Broken plasterwork was replicated, ceiling paintings restored, paint and ornaments
renewed. Three surgeries – one with a recovery room – were created on two levels. They
were executed as room-in-room architecture, leaving the view of the ceiling open and
maintaining visual separation from the historical decor by the use of transparent glazing.
At the same time, the gleaming surfaces and glass elements bring reflections into play
that visually enlarge the ballroom fragment.

Gallery surgery (above), new installations (below)

Stiller Dental Practice

Brahmsstrasse 11   GFA 120 m²   **wiewiorra hopp schwark architekten**   Client: PD Dr Dr Michael Stiller
14193 Berlin   GV   360 m³   www.whs-architekten.de

Wall fixture with wardrobe, reception desk and office entrance

Floor plan

Dental practice interior fittings in Berlin's Grunewald district. The key element is a wooden artefact consisting of irregularly shaped panels with dark joints. The folded wall fixture extends from the refurbished waiting room to the hall and on into the surgery. When closed, its heavily-grained, walnut veneer surface conceals both the cloakroom and reception desk that it houses and the rooms beyond: office, kitchenette and x-ray room. At the same time, with its internal fittings of black MDF panels, it introduces a dark accent into a bright ambience characterised by terrazzo floors and fabric wall coverings. The waiting room also serves as a seminar room from time to time. A screen built into the wall fixture enables direct transmissions from the adjacent surgery for training purposes.

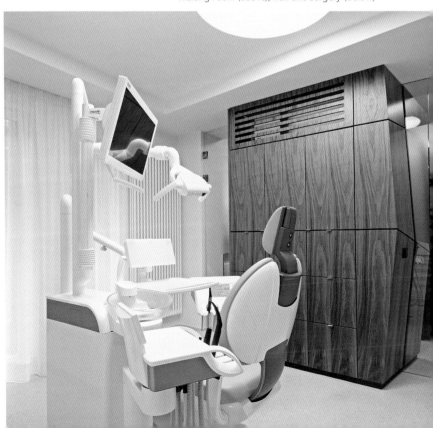

Waiting room (above), hall and surgery (below)

Stephanus-Stiftung – Building 8

| Parkstrasse 19 | GFA 975 m² | **Hüffer.Ramin** | Client: Stephanus-Stiftung |
| 13086 Berlin | GV 3,350 m³ | www.hueffer-ramin.de | |

Shop

Interim expansion status

Final design

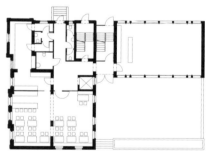

Ground floor plan

Conversion and expansion of an 1874 building into workshops for people with disabilities. The old building is part of a listed ensemble. In coordination with the preservation authorities, previous additions with staggered heights were replaced by a new extension. It is connected by an external staircase that maintains the floor levels of the old building, where the staff works in a café on the ground floor. There is a ceramics workshop on the first floor and a weaving workshop on the second. Goods produced in the workshops are sold on the ground floor of the new building. The two floors planned above this shop will provide space for future offices.

Old building (above), café (below)

Observation Tower on the Ebenberg

Eutzinger Strasse
76829 Landau

GFA 200 m²
GV 1,025 m³

Swillus Architekten
www.swillusarchitekten.de

Client: Landesgartenschau
Landau 2015 gGmbH

View from the east

Viewing platform

New construction of a 21-metre-high observation tower as a result of the competition held for the Landau State Garden Show in 2011. The seven inclined tower sections reference the process of formation of the Upper Rhine trench. The structure of the larch wood façade underlines the process of tectonic tension that resulted in the rift valley. The tower is the southern endpoint of the Garden Show grounds, which taper off into a landscape ramp. In one direction the tower offers views over the town, the Garden Show site and all the way to the Palatinate Forest. In the other direction there are views of the Ebenberg nature reserve, a fragment of the original, unfarmed natural landscape of the plain, which connects to the south.

→ for more on the Garden Show site cf. project 64, pages 164/165

Larch wood façade (above), view with landscape ramp and tower stairs (below)

Ellbachseeblick – Barrier-free Viewing Platform

72270 Baiersbronn	GFA	140 m²	**PARTNERUNDPARTNER architekten**
	Height	8.5 m	www.partnerundpartner.com
	Length	32 m	

Client: Municipality of Baiersbronn

On-site assembly

View into the Ellbach valley

New construction of a viewing platform above the Ellbach valley near Baiersbronn. The structure was built with regional Douglas fir timber, which is particularly resistant to weathering. The existing trees on site were preserved: the platform winds between the trunks and over the edge of the hillside and widens with the expanding view over the heights and valleys of the Black Forest. The balustrade inclines slightly outward to emphasise this expansion. A bench along the way and a podium at the end of the platform provide seating. All wooden structural framework and platform basket elements were sawn with CNC equipment, preassembled in sections and bolted together on site.

Overall view (above), diagrams of deformation under normal forces and heavy loads (below)

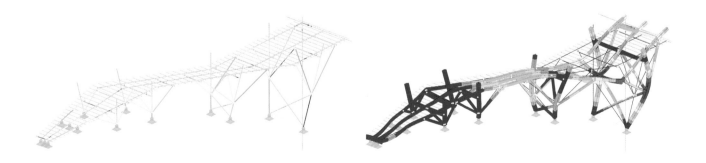

Bird's Nest for Children

Seestrasse 1
23992 Nakenstorf

Useable space 1 m²

Gernot Nalbach, Nalbach + Nalbach
Gesellschaft von Architekten mbH
www.nalbach-architekten.de

Client: Seehotel am Neuklostersee

Access side

New construction of a tree house for children. Concealed in the crowns of hazelnut trees, the nest was built on the grounds of a hotel on the banks of Neuklostersee lake. It can only be reached by a retractable rope ladder. The shell consists of willow branches. Inside, it is padded with soft Carex grass and provides space for two children. The braided structure is anchored to the trees with ropes.

Shell of willow branches (above), view from inside (below)

Multipurpose Hall at Rudolf Steiner School Berlin

Clayallee 104	GFA 1,250 m²	**Kersten+Kopp Architekten BDA**	Client: Rudolf Steiner Schule Berlin
14195 Berlin	GV 7,300 m³	www.kersten-kopp.de	

View from the northeast

Foyer

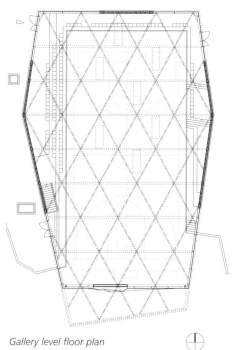

New construction of a sports and event hall on the campus of the Waldorf school in Berlin's Dahlem district. The hall is set into the slope: from the street, it appears to be single-storey, while it opens up to the playground with two-storey glazing. At the south side, the roof projects five metres, protecting a climbing wall. The changing room and hall level are reached via the foyer. On the other hand, visitor access to the stand is at street level. The design consists of a timber skeleton on a massive plinth. The loadbearing structure of walls and roof was built from domestic spruce. The façade is clad with untreated larch wood. A combined heat and power plant burns wood pallets to deliver heat to the new building.

Gallery level floor plan

View from the southwest (above), hall area (below)

Borgsdorf Sports Hall

Bahnhofstrasse 33b
16540 Hohen Neuendorf

GFA 2,400 m²
GV 14,500 m³

**Numrich Albrecht Klumpp
Gesellschaft von Architekten mbH**
www.nak-architekten.de

Client: City of Hohen Neuendorf

View from the southwest

New construction of a two-court hall as the final element of a school and sports centre under development since 1993. The court level is lowered. On the outside, the hall emerges with a band of windows running around three sides. Internal precast reinforced concrete V-supports carry the roof. A two-storey strip with stand, changing and ancillary rooms runs along the closed fourth side. The barrier-free hall structure uses 15 percent less energy than required by German law. Hot water is produced by a solar thermal system. A heat recovery system and energy-efficient LED lighting increase the energy efficiency.

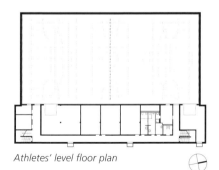

Athletes' level floor plan

Detail (top), stand (above), hall (below)

Johannes Kern School Sports Hall

Paul-Goppelt-Strasse 4
91126 Schwabach

GFA 2,975 m²
GV 19,700 m³

Heydorn Eaton
www.heydorneaton.de

Client: City of Schwabach

Corridor on the athletes' level

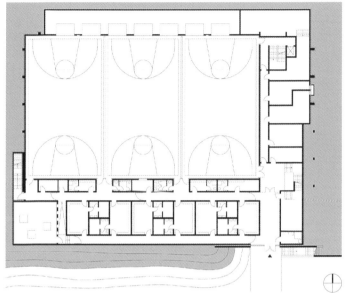

Athletes' level floor plan

New construction of a triple gymnasium as the result of a competition in 2010. The hall, which is designed as a wooden structure with glulam timber rafters, is used by both the Johannes Kern middle school and a neighbouring primary school. It was built on a terrace between the school and sports facilities. The changing, equipment and building services rooms are completely underground. Only the upper part of the actual hall and its stand protrudes above the ground as a pavilion. A band of windows running all round affords a view of the interior from all sides. The spectator entrance and foyer are at ground level on the east side. On the other hand, access to the actual hall is one level lower on the south side, where the subterranean athletes' area emerges through an incision in the slope.

View from the northwest (above), hall with stand (below)

Estádio Nacional Mané Garrincha

Asa Norte
70070-701 Brasília – DF
(Brazil)

GFA 120,000 m²

**gmp – Architekten
von Gerkan, Marg und Partner**
www.gmp-architekten.de

Client: Consórcio
Entap/Protende/Taiyo Birdair/Novacap

Overall view

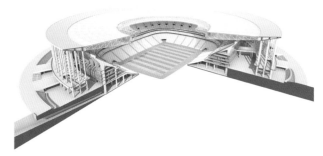

Schematic view

New construction of the national stadium in the Brazilian capital. This monumental landmark – now Brasília's largest single building – lies on the central axis of the city, which is part of the UNESCO World Heritage. gmp and the schlaich bergermann und partner engineering office jointly developed the circular esplanade containing all access elements. Three circles of columns support the double-shelled suspended roof. Castro Mello Arquitetos were responsible for planning the actual, 72,000-spectator capacity stadium bowl. The office had already designed the 1974 predecessor stadium in the same location.

Esplanade

Oliver G. Hamm

A city-centre campus

When will Berlin's Technical University embrace its surroundings?

For more than 130 years Berlin's Technical University (TU Berlin) has dominated Charlottenburg's eastern areas. Following the devastations of World War II, it was announced in April 1946 that the campus would be rebuilt on the block of land bordered by Strasse des 17. Juni, Hardenbergstrasse and Fasanenstrasse. Soon this triangular parcel proved insufficient and five new buildings were constructed to the east of Fasanenstrasse between 1954 and 1957 to accommodate the expanding university. From 1960 onwards, the campus spilled over onto the neighbouring block (also more or less triangular in shape) bordered by Marchstrasse, Einsteinufer and Strasse des 17. Juni. There, an ensemble of solitary structures was erected, largely positioned at right angles to each other, around a green centre. On the main campus the Institute for Mining and Metallurgy was built on Ernst-Reuter-Platz (1955–1959), and in 1965 additions were made to the university's main building (1884) including a high-rise extension and an adjoining auditorium.

Since the early 1970s further development has largely been limited to smaller additions to existing structures. A small number of new structures have joined the original ensemble; these include the Faculty of Physics (now the Eugene Paul Wigner Building) on the main campus (1972), the Mathematics Building (1976–1983) and the Centre for Electron Microscopy (2009–2011) on the northern site, and the university library on the Eastern Campus (completed in 2004). The Senate eventually commissioned the preparation of a master plan with the aim of more efficiently steering further development, enhancing links between the business, science and cultural sectors, and facilitating the integration of the campus within the surrounding city. The master plan, developed by Gruppe Planwerk, Fugmann Janotta and Nieto Sobejano Arquitectos, was presented in March 2009 and adopted by the Senate in August of the same year.

The *Masterplan Uni Campus City West* defines the central concepts underpinning developments on campus and locates renovation and modernisation projects, new builds and open spaces, as well as providing a structural overview of the intended land usage, including impacts on public space. The plan identifies impacted areas across the entire area bordered by Bahnhof Zoo, the Stadtbahn viaduct, Hardenbergstrasse, Marchstrasse and Landwehr Canal, with existing structures affected across most of the northern site and parts of the main campus, and new builds located primarily on the eastern campus site and on the outskirts of the northern campus site. Six years have passed since the adoption of the plan, yet little has changed on the campus. Moreover, some aspects of the plan have become outdated or require reconsideration. The planned construction of a research centre for engineering and computer science on Strasse des 17. Juni has, for instance, since been abandoned. This, despite the fact that the project was the subject of a competition – won by an ambitious design presented by Schulz & Schulz (Leipzig) – as recently as 2009. In the place of this the Technical University has secured leases for existing buildings, one of them on Marchstrasse with the option to purchase the building after 20 years.

The former Telefunken Building by Schwebes & Schoszberger on Ernst-Reuter-Platz (left), fenced-in campus on Fasanenstrasse (above)

Plans for the second major new build and the expansion of the campus on the eastern site are still far from final. In 2011 the extension of the campus was the subject of a planning competition that was decided in favour of a design presented by yellow z urbanism architecture and bgmr landscape architects. Their design proposed the creation of a "robust spatial framework" of existing and new structures on the eastern campus site and the relocation of a high-traffic bus terminus. With the adoption of the master plan developed on this basis, the utilisation of this site for research purposes was established under planning law.

Then, in 2013, Berlin architect Jan Kleihues independently presented a plan for six residential and commercial high-rise buildings – a plan that met with praise from Michael Müller, then Urban Development Senator and now Governing Mayor of Berlin. The development of the eastern campus site has been on hold ever since. In early 2015 an investor acquired a plot originally chosen as the site for a giant Ferris wheel (the project was shelved in 2010) after the Senate had declined to reacquire it. It remains to be seen whether this will breathe new life into the planning process.

The TU plans to build a new mathematics building on the eastern site to replace the dilapidated building on Strasse des 17. Juni. In addition to this, the university has applied for funding for the construction of a research facility and hopes to build another one later on. The German Aerospace Centre (DLR) also intends to build on this site. In addition to the mathematics building, the master plan identifies sites for other university buildings and structures for scientific institutions, with the aim of creating a vibrant urban district. The implementation of this plan – four years after it was presented – would require that a consensus be reached between the Senate and the boroughs of Mitte and Charlottenburg-Wilmersdorf (the boundary between these boroughs cuts across the site diagonally), the participating investors, and interested users.

The mathematics building is one of four projects at the university funded through a state-level investment programme that are to be implemented by 2027. The other three projects concern the redevelopment of the Seestrasse Campus in Wedding, the refurbishment of the façade on the technical chemistry building and asbestos abatement work at the Eugene Paul Wigner Building. The renovation and redevelopment of

*Winning design from the urban planning competition for the eastern
site by bgmr Landschaftsarchitekten and yellow z urbanism (left),
the Mathematics Building by Georg Kohlmaier and Barna von Sartory
from 1983 (right), the bus terminus on Hertzallee with the library building
by Lothar Jeromin and Walter A. Noebel in the background (below)*

existing buildings on campus is expected to take centre-stage
in the coming years. This will include the refurbishment of the
halls within the main building, according to a design by HAAS
Architekten – although a range of heritage conservation issues
are yet to be clarified.

The redevelopment of buildings erected in the 1950s through
to the 1970s has been the focus of work in recent years, with
remarkable results: the Telefunkenhochhaus (1958–1960)
on Ernst-Reuter-Platz was completely renewed according to
plans by na Architekten in a project spanning several phases
between 2005 and 2010. The same agency was responsible
for the renovation (2006–2013) of the high-rise building housing the Institute for Mining and Metallurgy, containing, among
other things, the TU's mineralogical collection. At present, the
adjoining low-rise building is refurbished for use by the TU's
new business incubator and a café. At the turn of 2012/2013,
Building L (built in 1955 as the Institute of Food Chemistry) on
the eastern campus was presented to the departments of bio-
chemistry and bio-catalysis following the completion of renova-
tions by Fissler Ernst Architects.

Diverse scientific and cultural services and events provide access
points for research institutions, enterprises, artistic initiatives
and the public. Still, the campus harbours as yet untapped
potentials for further development. The central and northern
campus sites leave a lot to be desired at present in terms of
their functional and aesthetic qualities. Particularly the open
spaces close to the existing structures have significant design
flaws. In addition to this, accessing green spaces and navigat-
ing the campus frequently proves to be a challenge for visitors.
The adoption of a landscaping master plan for the open spaces
could eliminate such defects.

At least work is now scheduled to begin in early 2016 on the
development of a section of the main campus bordering Hertzallee – a recently extended thoroughfare providing access to
the TU and to Universität der Künste. Adopted in autumn 2014
following a planning competition, this design by Lavaland and
TH Global will see the pathway running from Fasanenstrasse
through to Ernst-Reuter-Platz paved with granite and flanked
by trees. A number of areas along the revitalised corridor will
be widened to create plazas. This open area development
promises to transform the green heart of the campus into a
genuinely urban space rich in opportunities for interaction and
experience.

Public Library in the Old Fire Station

Michael-Brückner-Strasse 9 12439 Berlin	GFA (new building) GFA (existing structure) GV (new building) GV (existing structure)	1,875 m² 910 m² 7,325 m³ 3,450 m³	**Chestnutt_Niess Architekten BDA** www.chestnutt-niess.de	Client: State of Berlin represented by the Treptow-Köpenick Borough Council

View from the street

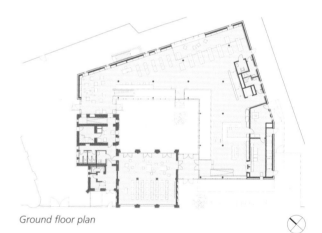

Ground floor plan

Conversion and enlargement of a listed 1912 fire station for a public library in Niederschöneweide. Two sides of the new building wrap around the historical monument and create a reading courtyard that is also accessible from the event room in the old fire engine hall. The station tower becomes the hub and pivot of the facility. The roof surfaces of the extension are inclined towards the old building. The ground and first floors are set back like galleries over the basement. Despite the old building, the complex uses 30 percent less energy than required by German law. The project was supported with financing from the European Fund for Regional Development (EFRE).

Fiction section in the basement (above), ground floor entrance area and reading courtyard (below)

Amadeu Antonio Community Education Centre

Puschkin-
strasse 13
16225
Eberswalde

GFA (new building)   1,200 m²
GFA (existing structure) 3,600 m²
GV (new building)   4,200 m³
GV (existing structure) 16,200 m³

Numrich Albrecht Klumpp
Gesellschaft von Architekten mbH
www.nak-architekten.de

Client: City of Eberswalde,
Amt für Hochbau und Gebäudewirtschaft

View from the street

Site plan with the extension (red) and
the original building (black hatching)

Library

Conversion and expansion of a listed school building. The 1892 girls' school received an extension in 1914, an addition in the 1950s and several later alterations. All of the time strata were brought together in this project. A new single-storey building complements the former L-shaped complex on the schoolyard side. This preserved the street frontage of the monument. A roof terrace was created on top of the new building, which accommodates a children's day care facility and public library. The citizens' hall, café and rooms for the administration and services of voluntary organisations round out the newly built community centre. A climate protection concept with heat contracting, which is now supplemented by a geothermal heat pump and a gas condensing boiler, ensures high energy efficiency.

New building with stairs to the roof terrace (above), café (below)

Letteallee Family Centre and Children's Day Care Facility

Letteallee 82–86
13409 Berlin

GFA (new building)   465 m²
GFA (existing structure) 190 m²
GV (new building)   1,325 m³
GV (existing structure) 740 m³

Chestnutt_Niess Architekten BDA
www.chestnutt-niess.de

Client: Kindertagesstätten Nordwest,
undertaking of the City of Berlin

Hall in the former chapel

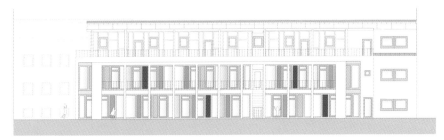

Courtyard façade colour scheme

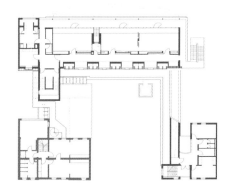

One-storey addition to a children's day care facility and conversion of a 1902 listed building in Reinickendorf into a family centre. Fixtures were removed from the former rectory to regain the original geometry of the chapel; cast-iron columns and masonry were exposed. The family centre can make use of the resulting space in different ways. It is divided into the cafeteria, a large open hall, an office and a meeting room. The low-rise day care building received an additional floor that houses more group rooms. The project was supported with financing from the European Fund for Regional Development (EFRE).

Upper (top) and ground floor plans

Corridor in the added storey

A Hut for the Tiger

Lübecker Strasse 13
10559 Berlin

GFA 22 m²
GV 68 m³

motaleb architekten
www.motaleb.de

Client: Kinderladen Tiger, Panther & Co.

Built-in cupboards

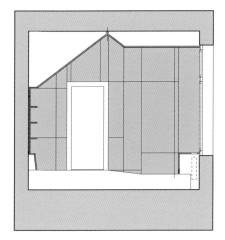

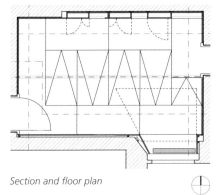

Section and floor plan

Redesign of a transitional space in a day care facility for infants. The Tiger, Panther und Co. facility uses a shop apartment on the mezzanine of Kurt Tucholsky's birthplace. A high, rectangular room had unpleasant acoustics and received only little daylight. The new interior fittings follow the idea of a primitive hut as a room within a room. Wooden surfaces and a light strip at the ridge create a bright atmosphere where children can occupy themselves as they wish and in ways different from the playroom. New storage space was built in the hut walls.

Overall view

German School in Madrid

Calle Monasterio de
Guadalupe 7
28049 Madrid
(Spain)

GFA 27,075 m²
GV 115,800 m³

Grüntuch Ernst Architekten
www.gruentuchernst.de

Client: Federal Office for Building
and Regional Planning

Foyer courtyard

New construction of a German school abroad with kindergarten, primary and secondary schools as the result of a competition in 2009. Each of the three buildings embraces a courtyard open to the landscape. The library, cafeteria, assembly/concert hall and sports hall are located on the south side of the school building. Foyer courtyards with perforated canopies combine every part into a quasi-organic framework. The foyer courtyard roofs protect from sun and heat. Their openings direct cool north wind into the courtyards. An underground thermal labyrinth and the pre-cooling of fresh air (by evaporative cooling of exhaust air) make active classroom air-conditioning unnecessary. A combined heat and power plant coupled with an absorption chiller, a gas condensing boiler and thermal and photovoltaic solar collectors are additional elements of the energy concept.

View of the secondary school from the east

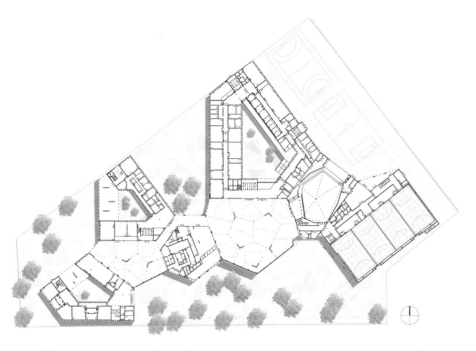

Ground floor plan (top), forecourt (above), internal courtyard (below)

Cafeteria at École Voltaire

Kurfürstenstrasse 53
10785 Berlin

GFA 510 m²
GV 1,750 m³

**Martin Schmitt Architektur /
Kommunikation im Raum**
www.m2sb.de

Clients: AEFE / École Voltaire Berlin

New construction of a cafeteria on the German-French school campus in Berlin's Tiergarten district. Part of the building rises to one storey, part to two, on a site under trees. The dining room, which can also be used for events, occupies large parts of the ground floor. The kitchen, serving counter and toilets are aligned on the west side, turned away from the schoolyard. Entrance and cloakroom are in the northeast section of the building. A second floor opens up as a gallery in the centre. This is the location of the teaching staff dining room. The elements for the wood frame building were precisely planned and prefabricated. Consequently, on-site assembly of the structure only required three weeks. The building is clad with heat-treated poplar battens over the insulation. The project received an Iconic Award from the German Design Council in 2015.

View from west (left), staircase to the gallery (above), teaching staff dining area (top)

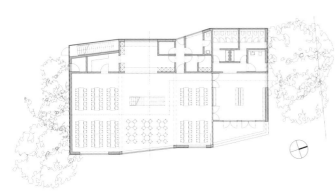

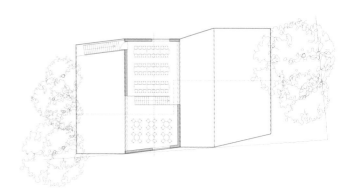

Ground (left) and upper floor plans

CHEGS Campus Staff Cafeteria

1st of July Rd 135
071051 Baoding
(China)

GFA 660 m²
GV 2,825 m³

KNOWSPACE /
Erhard An-He Kinzelbach Architekt BDA
www.knowspace.eu

Client: private

View from the north

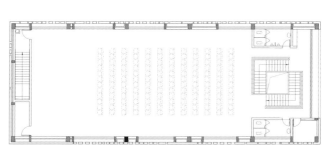

Ground (left) and upper floor plans

New construction on the campus of the state hydrogeological research institute.
The building dimensions were prescribed. It could not exceed the volume of a demolished brick hall that previously stood on this spot. This resulted in a two-storey building that appears monolithic from a distance. The kitchen and dining hall are located on the ground floor and a multipurpose hall was built above. It serves as an event space, but is also used for staff leisure activities. Large glass windows form the actual, inner façade. A 22-centimetre-thick, self-supporting granite façade is positioned in front of it – a reference to the institute's field of activity. At the same time, the perforation of this second shell is also a reminder of Chinese clay brick buildings for drying raisins. It ensures good ventilation and varying illumination of the building interior.

View at night (above), double winding stairs and multipurpose hall (below)

University of Kassel Campus Centre

Moritzstrasse 18
34127 Kassel

GFA 10,600 m²
GV 61,000 m³

raumzeit Gesellschaft von Architekten mbH
www.raumzeit.org

Client: State of Hesse represented by
Hessian Construction Management

Lecture room 1

New construction of a lecture hall and campus centre as the result of a competition in 2008. Six lecture theatres and six seminar rooms, with a total of 2,700 seats, were built in the interior. The position of the multi-storey halls can be read from the sculpted façade outside. In addition, university and student union offices, counselling and service facilities are housed in the centre. The new building is located between three plazas. The foyer, which can also be used as an event space and is open to all floors, is therefore accessible from several sides.

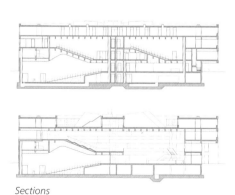

Sections

View from the north (above), foyer and ground floor plan (below)

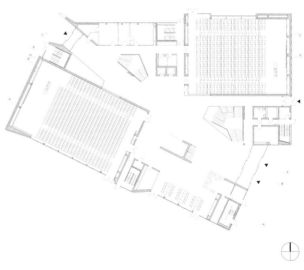

Zeppelin University ZF Campus

Fallenbrunnen 3
88045
Friedrichshafen

GFA (new building) 7,400 m²
GFA (existing structure) 9,500 m²
GV (new building) 27,400 m³
GV (existing structure) 38,000 m³

as-if Architekten
www.as-if.info

Client: Zeppelin University Friedrichshafen

Intersection of the old building and the roof terrace

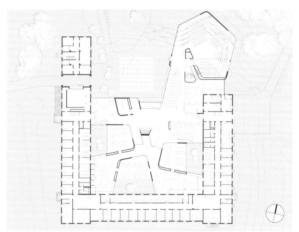

Ground floor plan

Patio

Modernisation and expansion of a barracks complex into a university building. The project is the result of a competition in 2010. The characteristic form of the old, U-shaped building from the 1930s was preserved. It houses offices and smaller work-rooms. A two-storey addition with a roof terrace fills the former courtyard. At its north-east end, it merges with the head-end building of the Forum (the university's largest lecture hall), which is one storey taller. The new building accommodates larger seminar rooms, the cafeteria and the library. At the same time, it serves as the hub of the entire complex. Its open spaces flow into transitions to the old building. On the north side, the Forum and its counterpart, the longer wing of the old building, frame an entrance plaza. As the centrepiece of the campus, it is used for events.

View of the Forum from the entrance plaza (above), main staircase, Forum and hall outside seminar room (below, clockwise)

Centre for Media – Mittweida University of Applied Sciences

Bahnhofstrasse 16
09648 Mittweida

GFA 14,900 m²
GV 59,000 m³

Georg Bumiller
Gesellschaft von Architekten mbH
www.bumillerarchitekten.de

Client: Free State of Saxony, Staatsbetrieb Sächsisches Immobilienmanagement / Chemnitz branch

Stair hall

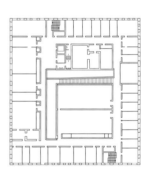

Stair hall

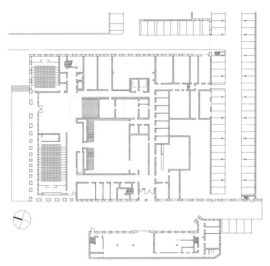

Ground (left) and upper floor plans

New building for the media and social work faculties. The building closes a gap on a street south of the actual campus. The compact structure is set back from the street. This resulted in a forecourt that gives access to the foyer. From there, an open stairway leads up to the atrium, which in turn gives access to the roof terrace on the attached parking deck. The core of the building is the large television studio, which is screened from noise by a ring of teaching and research rooms. Lecture halls and seminar rooms in this ring are oriented toward the street. The sound insulation is reinforced by the massive construction of the new building. The loadbearing façade consists of precast concrete units. The lintels and columns are set into each other in a way that makes the building appear to taper from floor to floor.

Main entrance on the street (above), television studio and façade detail (below)

Centre of Biomolecular Drug Research (BMWZ)

Schneiderberg 38	GFA	4,525 m²	**BHBVT Gesellschaft von Architekten mbH**
30167 Hannover	GV	19,050 m³	www.bhbvt.de

Client: State Construction
Management, Hannover

Laboratory

Corridor

Stairs

New building for a research centre at Leibniz Universität in Hannover. In shape and size, this building on the edge of the campus follows the master plan specifications. A recess at the west end of the ground floor marks the entrance. Together with an empty opening on the third floor, this recess provides a focus for the otherwise monolithic building. The façade's rhythm and material are decisive for the outward appearance. The staggering of the windows continues around the gable. The surfaces of the perforated façade consist of glass mosaic. They are ceramic coated on the rear and therefore change in colour, depending on the incident light. Internally, laboratories and workrooms face each other to assure short paths. These rows are only interrupted by occasional widening of the corridors, which is expressed externally by bays.

View from the northeast (above), site plan und ground floor plan (below)

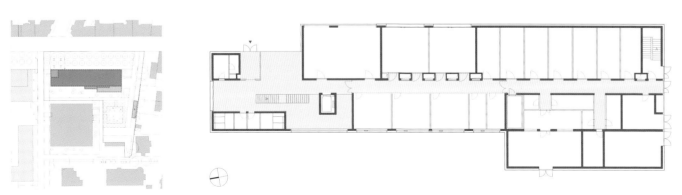

BAM Laboratory Building

Richard-Willstätter-Strasse 11
12489 Berlin

GFA 14,075 m²
GV 61,375 m³

kleyer.koblitz.letzel.freivogel
gesellschaft von architekten mbh
www.kklf.de

Client: Federal Office for Building
and Regional Planning

Foyer in the conference area

Laboratory façade with technology centre

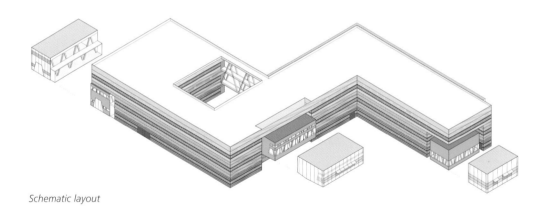

Schematic layout

New building for the Federal Institute for Materials Research and Testing (BAM) as the result of a competition in 2006. The meandering building complements two existing structures to form an institute campus. To this end, it continues the right-angled development of the Adlershof science and technology park. This results in an entrance courtyard that gives access to every building and a garden courtyard one side of which is closed by a bridge structure between the building wings. Three special structures are integrated into the new building: a technology centre and an area for NMR spectroscopy (magnetic resonance) at the head ends and a conference room above the entrance. Inside the three-layered wings, offices are aligned on one side, laboratories on the other and storage, service areas and media shafts are placed between them.

View of the entrance (above), garden courtyard and conference room (below)

Building emotions

Modernism couldn't exist without its sidekick, Expressionism

The entrance to Ossip Klarwein's 1934 church on Hohenzollernplatz (left), apartment block on Spandauer See by Krüger Schuberth Vandreike, 1998 (above)

Among contemporary architects it is commonly held that the profession requires an artistic sensibility. It is all the more surprising then, that their work has so little in common with contemporary visual arts. Formally, conceptually and philosophically, architects and artists live in two different worlds. Even percent-for-art projects – here in Germany a predominantly government-funded exercise – possess an attributive character and do not speak to the architecture as such.

It was not like that a hundred years ago. Art Nouveau architects and adherents of the emerging Modernist movement – many of whom were artists themselves – maintained close ties within the various contemporary art scenes. The decorative systems employed within the context of Art Nouveau spanned multiple disciplines. In the case of Russian Constructivism and *De Stijl* in the Netherlands, innovations in the colouration and segmentation of edifices were driven by developments in the respective art scenes. Likewise, Expressionism – the artistic successor to Impressionism – was itself taken up by architects. In Germany, figures like the Taut brothers, Wenzel Hablik and Hans Scharoun established various organisations, such as the *Arbeitsrat für Kunst* and *Gläserne Kette*, employing group dynamics to create visionary architectural designs that were true expressions of emotion.

The majority of architects were probably more prosaic in their outlook. But as they cast about in search of a new style following neo-Historicism's descent into eclecticism and its subsequent demise, the vocabulary of Expressionism had a particular appeal as it could so easily be transposed into architecture. Triangles and acute angles were more rational forms of expression, and circles and ovals remained the exception in Expressionist art and architecture.

Behind these ambitions lay an awareness that buildings could be expressive works of art, perhaps even capable of replacing painting. "Buildings are full of life," wrote the art historian Heinrich de Vries in 1920. "As works of art, they are one step closer to the infinite, taking us nearer to the end of painting as an art form in its own right, supplanted by the much greater expressiveness of architecture."

Of course, in practice Expressionist forms had by and large a decorative function, and right angles remained the norm in floor plans and rising walls. One exception here was Erich Mendelsohn's sculptural Einsteinturm. Other architects used brick to create a sense of three-dimensionality in their façades; they included Fritz Höger, who worked mainly in Hamburg but also designed a number of buildings in Berlin; Reichspost architect Karl Pfuhl, who built the Reichspostzentralamt on Ringbahnstrasse; and German Bestelmeyer, builder of the Reichsschuldenverwaltung on Oranienstrasse. These architects used reliefs as linking motifs, along with special tile formats and coloured glazes, to create highly textured façades that in many cases distracted the eye from the inherent plasticity of the building itself.

The parallels with Brick Gothic are apparent in the use of pilasters, cornices, battlements and other elements of ornamentation, including symbolic sculptures such as those seen at the Reichsschuldenverwaltung. Not surprisingly, churches provide some

of the greatest examples of Expressionist architecture. One of the finest is the church on Hohenzollernplatz, built between 1931 and 1933 by Ossip Klarwein of Fritz Höger's practice; the building's simple, disciplined layout, thrusting narrow ribs and sharply pointed arches seemingly striving to outdo Gothic architecture's heavenly aspirations. Even more exalted is St Michael's in Wannsee, Berlin's first Expressionist church, with its three pointed spires, built by Wilhelm Fahlbusch in 1927. And then of course there is the opulent Kreuzkirche on Hohenzollerndamm in Schmargendorf, with its Asian-style wedding hall decorated with colourful glazed ceramic tiles, built in 1930 by Ernst and Günter Paulus.

Berlin is rich in buildings from this period. Niels Lehmann and Christoph Rauhut recently anthologised this precious heritage in their book *Fragments of Metropolis – Berlins expressionistisches Erbe*. They include many power stations, and in particular the substations built all over Berlin by Hans Heinrich Müller, the architect at the electricity company Bewag. His counterpart at the Reichsbahn, Richard Brademann, was another important figure in this respect, responsible for a large number of rectifier stations for the S-Bahn and a series of Expressionist-styled train stations, including an especially picturesque example at Wannsee.

Other pioneering architects included Eugen Schmohl, whose two ultramodern reinforced concrete skyscrapers, the Borsigturm (1922 to 1924) and the Ullsteinhaus (1924 to 1926), used the vocabulary of Expressionist brickwork to avoid breaking character with an overly avant-garde design. In short, they respected their clients' wish for dignity and historical continuity, but used a new and different formal repertoire.

While historic styles, with their columnar orders and rounded arches, were virtually anathema to modern architects, the transition from Expressionism to Rationalism was a smooth one – not least because many members of the profession spanned both genres during their careers. Figures such as Peter Behrens, Bruno and Max Taut, Walter Gropius and Hans Scharoun were outstanding exponents first of Expressionism, and then of Neue Sachlichkeit. (Some critics even regard Scharoun's postwar Philharmonie and Staatsbibliothek as a return to Expressionism.) As a result, the use of Expressionist motifs declined only gradually, and they continued to be applied referentially in many Modernist buildings. Some were incorporated into the repertoire of the International Style and still make their presence felt today.

While columns, porticoes, and round and pointed arches are relatively uncommon these days – one example being David Chipperfield's monumental round-arched façade beside the Ebertbrücke on Tucholskystrasse – Expressionism remains a point of reference in contemporary architecture. The house built by Krüger Schuberth Vandreike in 1998 on the Schultheiss site in Spandau, with its folded façade and zigzag eaves, is rightly considered an example of Brick Expressionism in its contemporary form.

Scharnhorst electrical substation by Hans Heinrich Müller, 1928 (left), Femina-Palast by Bielenberg & Moser, 1931, and Mossehaus, rebuilt in 1921–1923 by Erich Mendelsohn (right), Scholz & Friends headquarters by Müller Reimann Architekten, 2011 (below)

But perhaps the most important protagonist at the interface of Modernism and Expressionism was Erich Mendelsohn. His Einsteinturm in Potsdam, with its flowing, wavelike curves, did not have a significant impact on architecture at the time of its construction. The edifice was troubled by technical flaws and Mendelsohn did not pursue the idea further, though its sculptural vision is echoed today in the signature architecture of Zaha Hadid and Coop Himmelb(l)au. At a stretch, the bubble-like motifs on Jürgen Mayer H.'s façades on Johannisstrasse might also be viewed in this context.

It was Mendelsohn's elegant use of lines to add movement to modern, Rationalist buildings that appealed most because it was so easy to copy. The Mossehaus and the Schaubühne on Lehniner Platz are among the few surviving buildings of this kind built by Mendelsohn in Berlin. The Titania-Palast, built in 1928 by Jacobi, Schloenbach und Schöffler on Steglitzer Schlossstrasse, and the former Femina-Palast, constructed by Bielenberg & Moser in 1931 on Nürnberger Strasse, are in the same vein. Corner windows, and prominent cornices enclosing bands of windows, still appear today in buildings such as the Cubix Kino on Alexanderplatz, by nps tchoban voss, and the headquarters of advertising agency Scholz & Friends on Henriette-Hertz-Platz, by Müller Reimann Architekten.

Things have not changed that much since the 1930s. They had classic Modernist architecture dominated by white and glass cubes – and so do we. They had architects with an artistic sensibility who were not satisfied with this aseptic repertoire and used brick, travertine, rhombuses and parabolic arches to create buildings of character and atmosphere – and so do we. In their time these architects enjoyed widespread public admiration – as do their successors today.

Pforzheim Gasometer

Hohwiesenweg 6　　　GFA 3,200 m²　| **Aescht & Berthold Architekten**　　　Client: Parkhotel Pforzheim GmbH & Co. KG
75175 Pforzheim　　GV 53,825 m³　| www.aescht-berthold.de

Façade of the entrance building

Passageways

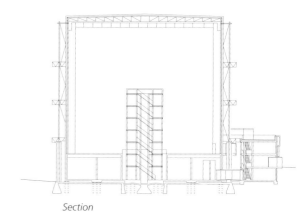

Section

Renovation of a listed historical gasometer from 1912 for the presentation of 360° panoramic images. A new entrance building on the eastern face of the gasometer houses the facility's ticketing centre, shop, café, wardrobe, toilets, and utility rooms on three levels. Its rooftop has been designed for use as a terrace. The new building presents a closed façade of dark prefabricated concrete scales to the roadside. On the other side, a glass front in front of a multi-level lobby affords views of the historical structure. Passageways on two levels connect the new building with the gasometer, leading into an exhibition on the ground floor, and from the upper floor into the panorama hall above, in the centre of which a tower presents visitors with 360° views over multiple levels. The exhibition cylinder is clad with bright annealed stainless steel and rests within the historical framework.

View from the east (above), ground floor plan (below)

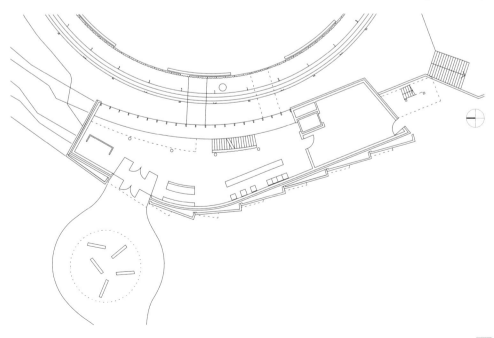

LWL Museum of Art and Culture

Domplatz 10　　　GFA 18,000 m²　　**Staab Architekten**　　　Client: Landschaftsverband Westfalen-Lippe
48143 Münster　　GV 92,850 m³　　www.staab-architekten.com

Museum tour on the upper floor

View from above with Domplatz

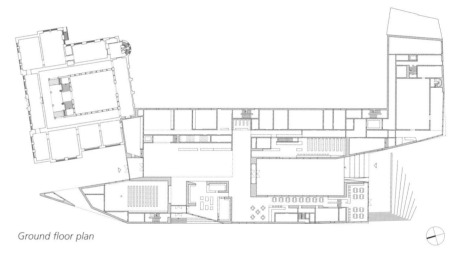

Ground floor plan

New building for an art museum as a result of a competition held in 2005. The building extends an existing neo-Renaissance structure built in 1908 and replaces a development from the 1970s. The ground floor (housing a library, events hall, eatery and book shop) can be accessed free of charge. Four public areas provide for a fluid transition from the city into the museum's interior. The centre is dominated by an atrium-style lobby, accessible for visitors coming from Johannisstrasse across a forecourt and connecting patio. A forecourt on Domplatz provides a second point of entry on this side. Generous windows structure the museum tour that includes the adjacent historical building. The new building's façades reflect the regional idiom with sandstone complemented by lighter concrete and plastered surfaces. The building has been certified through the EU GreenBuilding Programme.

New and old together (above), lobby (below)

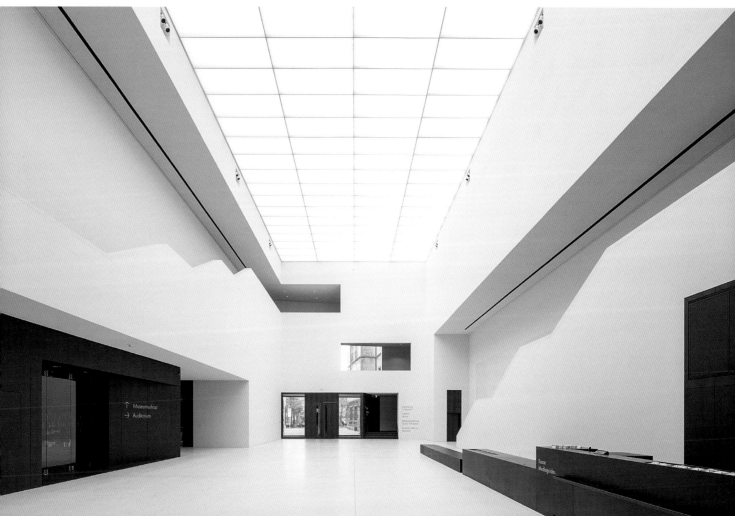

Württembergisches Staatstheater – Schauspielhaus

Oberer Schlossgarten 6　　GFA 7,800 m²　　**KLAUS ROTH architekten bda**　　Client: State of Baden-Württemberg
70173 Stuttgart　　　　　　GV　 41,500 m³　　www.klaus-roth.de　　　　　　　represented by Vermögen und Bau
　　Baden-Württemberg, Amt Stuttgart

The auditorium's sculptural structure

Modernisation and refurbishment of a theatre by architects Volkart, Perlia and Pläcking from 1962. The entire building – housing a stage, auditorium, lobbies and personnel facilities – has been restructured and refitted with state-of-the-art technology. A triangular-faced prismatic structure with a wenge finish overcomes the division between the auditorium's walls and ceiling. This sculptural folded structure, integrating 800 LED panels, has improved the acoustic qualities of the auditorium to a degree that renders on-stage amplification unnecessary. Seating was also raised to improve visibility. Outside the auditorium, the corridors have been refitted with oak panels. The bar, wardrobe, lounge, merchandising counter and ticketing desk form distinct islands within the lobby. The new aluminium and glass façade takes its cue from the building's original structure and window profiles.

View into the lobby

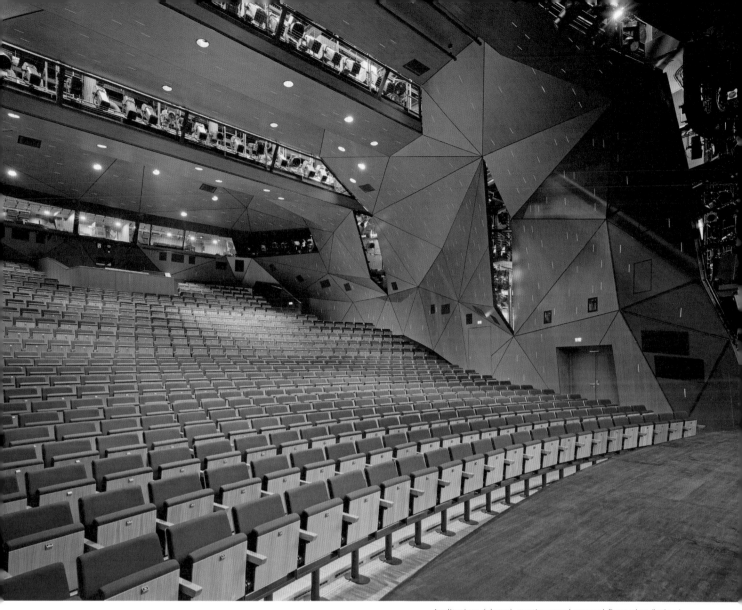

Auditorium (above), sections and ground floor plan (below)

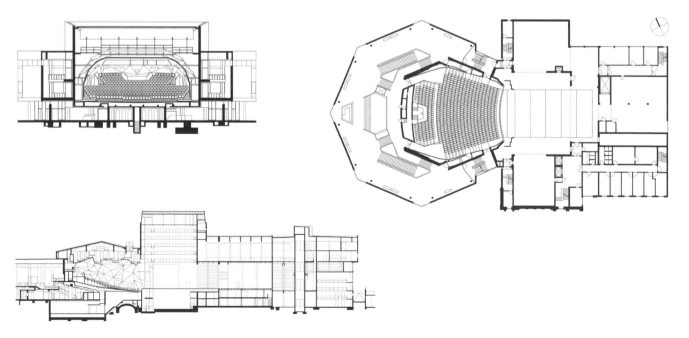

Chapel of the Dorotheenstadt Cemetery

Chaussee
strasse 126
10115 Berlin

GFA (new building)	27 m²
GFA (existing structure)	285 m²
GV (new building)	95 m³
GV (existing structure)	1,235 m³

Nedelykov Moreira Architekten
www.nedelykov-moreira.com

Client: Stiftung
Historische Kirchhöfe und Friedhöfe
Berlin Brandenburg, Evangelischer
Friedhofsverband Berlin Stadtmitte

Seating

New altar with integrated LED lighting

Light art by James Turrell

Refurbishment and modification of a cemetery chapel built in 1928. This site
is home to a listed and well-frequented historical cemetery. A host of leading intel-
lectuals and notables from the arts and culture have been laid to rest here over the
last 250 years – including Schinkel and Stüler, Hegel and Fichte, Brecht and Heartfield.
The chapel's interior underwent a radical overhaul in the 1960s. This latest refurbishment marks the second of three phases in the cemetery's ongoing development. An
annex with sanitary facilities and an access ramp were added to the chapel. The roof
and sections of the exterior surfaces were renewed, the windows extended through to
the floor, and the tympanum and doors glazed. Inside, the gallery was restored. Folda-
way backrests were fitted to the new, heated pews. With the generous support of a
sponsor, a light work by artist James Turrell has also been installed.

Exterior view (above) and interior (below) illuminated by the light art installation

Forest of Remembrance Memorial Site

Henning-von-Tresckow-Kaserne
Werderscher Damm 21
14548 Schwielowsee

GFA 125 m²
GV 580 m³

Rüthnick Architekten
www.ruethnick.com

Client: Federal Ministry of Defence, represented by Brandenburgischer Landesbetrieb für Liegenschaften und Bauen

Place of silence

Entrance building

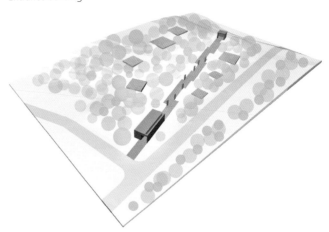

Visualisation

Construction of a memorial commemorating all members of the Bundeswehr killed in the line of duty. A central pathway of remembrance guides visitors to the site through an open entrance building and exhibition to a place of silent commemoration at the other end of the memorial. Seven steles flank the pathway on either side. The steles have been engraved with the names of the 104 soldiers who lost their lives in missions abroad to date. The pathway affords visitors views of seven individual memorials located in forest clearings at the site. These memorials, originally established in conflict zones, have been rebuilt on location using original elements and materials.

Pathway with steles

All waters

How many beavers does the inner city need?

The Spreepromenade at Kronprinzenbrücke in Berlin-Mitte (left), European beaver (Castor fiber) (above)

Rivers are woven into the fabric of Europe's urban history. Paris is synonymous with the Seine, Vienna with the Danube; even Venice has the Brenta, which feeds into the Grand Canal and the lagoon. But fifteen years ago, and largely unnoticed by the public, a new chapter began in the story of the continent's tamed urban rivers. In 2000 the European Union's framework water directive required member states to clean up their water bodies by 2027 – and that includes those flowing through cities.

Since then, a great deal of work has been done to restore them to pristine condition. This is a local and international challenge, because the directive bundles single rivers and streams into systems that transcend borders. It has created a huge and highly attractive market for landscape architects restoring biodiversity and reshaping riverbanks. Most of the recent German garden shows have been used by local authorities as opportunities to clean up neglected waterways, and although this is often a long and arduous task, the results have often been quite impressive.

One example is the picturesque town of Schwäbisch Gmünd, which used the 2014 Baden-Württemberg State Garden Show as a chance to realise a long-held dream. The Berlin firm A24 Landschaft restored the river Rems and one of its tributaries to their former status as the central focus of the townscape, raising the riverbeds by up to four metres, levelling the banks and redesigning the open spaces on the edge of the old town. Today, the view is one of rippling blue water rather than deep, gurgling gulleys. The idea is to bring rivers out into the open, not hide them away by canalising them. But some authorities face much bigger challenges than others, and this is partly down to size: generally speaking, the wider the river, the larger the task. Berlin started on a small scale, almost as a warmup for the major challenge ahead. It drew up development plans for its minor rivers, from the Panke to the Tegeler Fliess, and didn't begin work on the biggest, the Spree, until 2013. Here, it started with the less difficult eastern section, the Müggelspree. In the southwest of the city, the Spree and the Müggelsee are already a string of green pearls or rather: of nature reserves and Natura 2000 habitats. Not so the inner city, where a second factor comes into play: historic usage patterns. If a river becomes navigable, environmental and economic considerations come into conflict, because navigable rivers attract commercial settlement that radically reshapes them over the centuries. Historic usage becomes inseparable from urban integration, and industrial towns and cities originally built where rivers could be forded have particularly close relationships with the water. So existing settlement patterns are the third key factor determining the difficulty of river restoration.

Open spaces simplify the restoration process because they make it easier to let rivers take their own course. These areas tend to be located in suburban and outlying areas, and it is here that cities such as London, Paris, Hamburg and Berlin are starting the process of complying with the directive. There is much less scope for change in city centres. Although the directive demands significant environmental improvements, in a densely populated city these must be reconciled with other, equally important requirements, principal among which is preserving the existing urban structure. It's

so a project on the scale of Nijmegen is not going to happen. Berlin rather needs to ensure that the Spree gets enough water in times of climate change and the flooding of former surface mines in the Spreewald where much of it is stored. On the other hand, it needs to create storage space of a quite different type: by 2020, seventy thousand cubic metres of ditches and canals will be added to the combined sewer system, which regularly overflows into the Spree during heavy rains.

But no one would subscribe to the idea of a beaver's lodge next to the Reichstag: the Spree's course through the city centre is not up for negotiation. Instead, efforts are concentrating on three areas: reducing pollution, creating wildlife corridors, and making riverbanks accessible. If the river's natural assets are to be harnessed for the city's benefit, we may as well exploit its recreational potential. New promenades will ensure that the city starts interacting with the water. This is now possible because both 19th-century canalisation and legal measures in the 20th century aiming to reduce industrial pollution have helped to improve water quality.

Some parts of Berlin have started to turn to the water already some time ago. One example is Schöneweide, where waterways are staging a recovery following the decline of manufacturing. This happened even earlier in Moabit and Charlottenburg, and a whole new district has been slowly growing up around the Rummelsburger Bucht since the 1990s, centred on the water and fairly well integrated with the natural environment. A similar concept has been used on the Oberhavel in Spandau – less successfully, but the will is there. Even in the city centre, and along the Spree between Kreuzberg and Friedrichshain, the watchword today is that riverbanks are for everyone.

That's humans taken care of, but what about animals? In 2009, there was considerable excitement when a platform was built at great expense on the riverside, near the East Side Gallery, as a rest stop for beavers making the long and arduous swim through the city. The beavers were not impressed, and it was not until five years later, during the Christmas of 2014, that one of them took pity and left some teeth marks on a nearby willow. Berlin's beavers do have more pressing problems: rest stop or no rest stop, as far as they are concerned this is still a divided city. There are eastern beavers and western beavers, but so far it has been a case of never the twain shall meet. They have spread as far as the Rummelsburger Bucht to the east and Tiergarten to the west, and that's as far as it goes. Even if they could swim through the city with the help of more equally expensive rest stops, they would still have to get through the Mühlendammschleuse, the lock in central Berlin, a listed structure that's impassable to large rodents and many fish species.

In recent years, conservationists have built wildlife corridors to overcome such barriers. Berlin is committed to this idea of networked habitats, and the state's newly updated landscape

essential to review these in detail, which may require some stakeholders to take a less blinkered approach. The key question is to what extent the need for environmental and water management should overrule other considerations: in other words, how we reconcile the directive's requirements with factors such as design quality, preservation of the urban landscape, and the recreational benefits of parks and other outdoor spaces.

In itself, protecting the natural environment seems hardly ever enough to justify major changes to the built environment. The Dutch city of Nijmegen changed the course of the river Waal, redeveloping an area of 250 hectares and creating a new branch of the Rhine in the city centre. Here, protecting the environment is a pleasant side effect, but the main purpose of the project was flood protection. This is not a problem for Berlin,

*Landscaping of the Südpanke by bbzl böhm benfer zahiri landschaften städtebau (left),
the Josefsbach, a tributary of the Rems in Schwäbisch Gmünd, after landscaping
by A24 Landschaft (right), the Mühlendamm Lock – historic structure or beaver barrier? (below)*

programme even has designated particular species to focus on first, mobilising support for the wider concept. The idea is that if you create corridors for species like beavers and flowering rushes, less glamorous species of fauna and flora will profit as well. This is clever, but it highlights a fundamental dilemma: most people are not particularly interested in nature conservation unless there's something in it for them. Ideally, it should consolidate and increase the amount of land available for their own enjoyment, and have abundant stocks of fluffy animals and pretty flowers.

Take Munich, for example. Between 2000 and 2011, the Bavarian capital restored eight kilometres of the river Isar in what was probably Germany's most ambitious project of its kind. It wasn't just about conservation: it also had benefits in terms of flood protection and recreation. But as the weekly *Die Zeit* warned at the time, the project could be the victim of its own success. Clouds of barbecue smoke, thousands of nature enthusiasts and frolicking dogs will not exactly create an idyllic environment for kingfishers and white-throated dippers.

If we are not careful, the renaissance of urban rivers could have big drawbacks. Even if we agree that rivers are an asset, there

will be conflicting interests to reconcile. The more attractive the rivers become, the more people will want to come and enjoy them, while others will try to stop them. And Berlin is no exception.

We had a foretaste of this in the summer of 2015, when Hermann Parzinger, president of the Stiftung Preussischer Kulturbesitz, objected to plans for an outdoor swimming pool in the river on the Museumsinsel. The project, funded by the federal and state governments and designed by realities:united, will have the added benefits of cleaning up the water and creating new ecosystems. The idea is that the Kupfergraben canal could become a clean tributary of the Spree, with a tank of reeds, aquatic plants and gravel beds being used to filter the river water before it enters the swimming pool. The upper reaches of the canal on the Fischerinsel will be restored to create a nature reserve and waterside park, providing a stepping stone within the city centre and practically halving the distance between habitats on the river.

The downside of all this, Parzinger claimed, was that it would attract crowds of noisy people and piles of litter. People should be "immersing themselves in art" rather than swanning around in river water and endangering the status of a UNESCO world heritage site. Will Kupfergraben follow in the footsteps of Dresden's Waldschlösschenbrücke, the controversial bridge whose construction led UNESCO to delist the Elbe Valley?

Parzinger was not the only prominent figure to question the project's merits. A few weeks previously, in the daily newspaper *Die Welt*, architecture critic Dankwart Guratzsch slammed the pool idea, calling for the city's historic built environment to be protected. Instead of greening everything in sight, he said, managing the city's density was still the best way of ensuring that human settlement was compatible with the natural environment. Guratzsch could have used a better example than the swimming-pool project to question the idea of greener cities, but he has a point. If we are serious about looking after nature and the environment, we must radically rethink our relationship with both. And that may mean being able to manage without seeing beavers everywhere we look.

Restored Isar in Munich (left), artist's impression of the filter section of the Berlin outdoor swimming pool project by realities:united (above) and plan of the whole project (below)

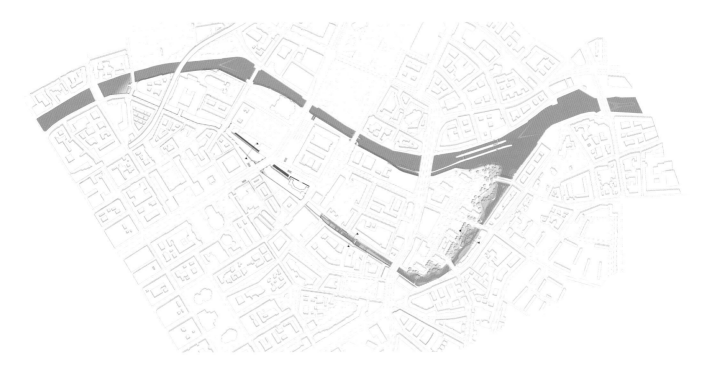

Ottoplatz

50679 Cologne | Area 7,000 m² | **bbzl – böhm benfer zahiri landschaften städtebau** www.bbzl.de | Client: City of Cologne, Amt für Straßen und Verkehrstechnik

Overall view

Redevelopment of a public square outside a train station, commissioned following a limited competition. The square is located at the front of the listed entrance building to the Cologne Messe/Deutz train station from 1914. The square is flanked by several buildings of very different appearance. A surface of natural stone sets the square off from its surroundings and lends visual coherence to the overall architectural context. Newly planted trees seal gaps on the square's boundary line. The square itself has been elevated above its surroundings by two steps. Two 25-metre-long seating islands of concrete define the scene. Together they form a line, positioned either side of an opening opposite the dome and steps to the station building.

Detailing on the seating island

Seating island

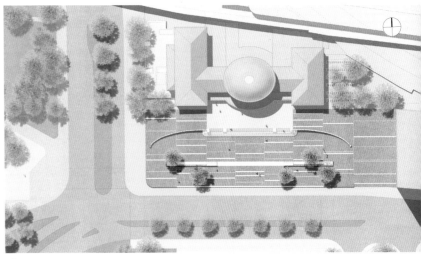

Plan

Market Square

06246 Goethestadt
Bad Lauchstädt

Area
11,075 m²

**WES LandschaftsArchitektur /
Hans-Hermann Krafft**
www.wes-la.de

Client: City of Goethestadt Bad Lauchstädt

Market square with fountain

Redevelopment of the market square and adjoining areas following a competition held in 2011. The market square is the central space where the narrow streets of this spa town converge. The square's natural stone cobbles were re-cut to improve pedestrian and vehicle access and safety, and historical surfaces were complemented by the addition of new, low-maintenance granite paving. Other new elements installed on the square include contemporary seating elements, a low-key lighting system and a small fountain opposite the free-standing town hall. The addition of trees outside the houses lining the square builds on local traditions.

Natural stone cobbles (above), trees and plan (below)

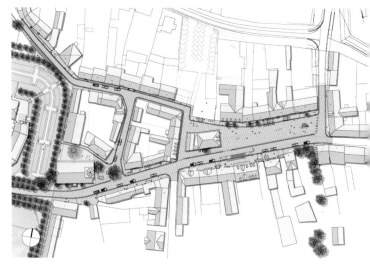

L'Île Verte

Rue de la Vigie 11	Area	**100Landschaftsarchitektur und GRUE**	Client: Lausanne Jardins 2014
1003 Lausanne	950 m²	www.100land.de	
(Switzerland)			

Bench with mint

Detail

Plan

Upgrade of municipal boules courts established in 1934. This project makes use of existing poles and railings to revitalise a neglected public space. These elements were painted in five shades of green and, through the addition of painted scaffolding poles, converted into seating benches and platforms. The five shades of green chosen for the project are mint, aniseed, asparagus, sage, and absinthe. Plantings of the corresponding species enhance the scenery: mint, aniseed, asparagus, sage and wormwood (from which absinthe is distilled). On the western side a flight of steps was cleared of undergrowth and restored to use, providing additional access. Originally conceived as a temporary project for the municipal Lausanne Jardins festival, the project has been extended by the authorities, who plan to continue the plantings and restoration work.

Painted fence (above), new grandstand (below)

Schillerpark

Bristolstrasse
13349 Berlin

Area
26,000 m²

**TOPOS Stadtplanung
Landschaftsplanung Stadtforschung**
www.topos-planung.de

Client: Mitte Borough Council, Berlin

Lime tree circle

Promenade on Bristolstrasse

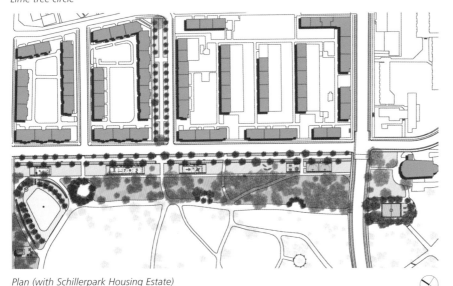

Plan (with Schillerpark Housing Estate)

Restoration of the north-western boundary of the historical park. This site lies within the buffer zone surrounding Schillerpark Housing Estate, a UNESCO World Heritage location. Throughout this project new pathways were laid within the park, plantings renewed and a circle of lime trees restored. The park's historical water playground from 1910 was completely overhauled, ensuring that it meets modern hygiene standards without altering its appearance. Toilet stalls on site were converted into a world heritage information kiosk and café. The southern lane of the adjoining road (Bristolstrasse) was converted to a green space with playing grounds and a walkway bordering the park. The median strip was remodelled to form a tree-lined promenade. The project was conducted in consultation with conservation authorities in Berlin and funded with the support of the Investment Programme for National UNESCO World Heritage Sites.

Water playground (above), playing grounds on Bristolstrasse (below)

Schmalkalden State Garden Show

98574 Schmalkalden

Area
74,000 m²

**sinai Gesellschaft
von Landschaftsarchitekten mbH**
www.sinai.de

Clients: Landesgartenschau Schmalkalden
2015 GmbH, Municipality of Schmalkalden
and Landratsamt Schmalkalden-Meiningen

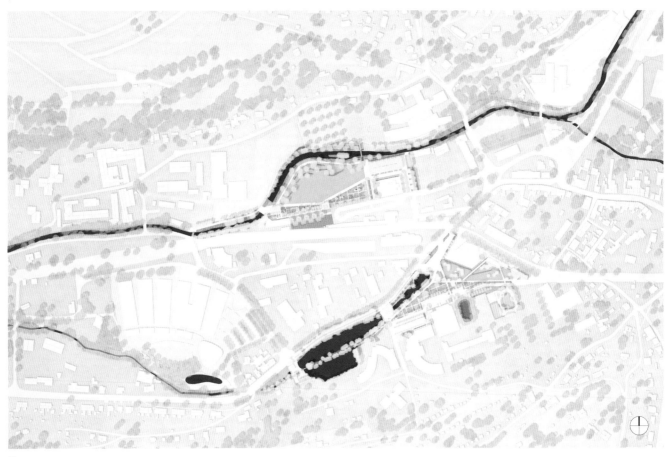

Plan

Walkway across the ponds

Landscape design for two new parks created following a competition in 2010. The spatial sequences of the parks connect the sites of this formerly purely commercial neighbourhood and revitalise the western borders of the town's historical centre. The parks share a common vocabulary of materials and details, coupled with a border of grasses and shrubbery complemented by columnar trees. Despite this, each park has a particular identity: the Westend Park frames the newly restored banks of the Schmalkalde River with its lawn terraces and a grassy meadow offers plenty of space for large-scale events. At the Stadtpark, walkways across the pond provide access to a new promenade flanking the pond that feeds the Fuchsenkothe. Playgrounds in the planted borders connect the park with neighbouring schools.

The source of the Fuchsenkothe (above), Schmalkalde in Westend Park (below)

Conversion of the Estienne et Foch Garrison

Georg-Friedrich-Dentzel-Strasse 1
76829 Landau in der Pfalz

Area
270,000 m²

A24 Landschaft Landschaftsarchitektur GmbH
www.a24-landschaft.de

Client: Landesgartenschau
Landau 2015 gGmbH

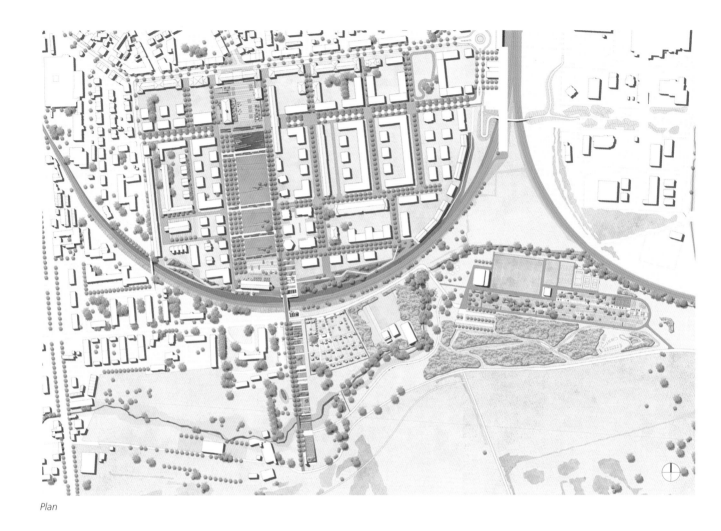

Plan

Creation of new open spaces for the 2015 Rhineland-Palatinate State Garden Show. The commission follows a competition held in 2011. These green spaces lend structure to the new residential suburb established on the site of this former military facility. With its lusciously planted pond, the Park of Generations is the centrepiece of this conversion. A green ribbon guides the eye along the park's perimeter from the city out into the countryside. The ribbon reflects regional traditions in cultural landscape planting and ends at a ramp leading to the observation tower on the rim of the Ebenberg Natura 2000 area. A former coal depot lies to the east of the ribbon. The depot's platforms and yards are home to valuable ruderal vegetation and provide the backdrop for a sports and recreation campus with facilities for trend sports.

→ for more on the observation tower cf. project 35, pages 92/93

Seating

Pond at the Park of Generations

Ramp at the observation platform (above), skateboarding park (below)

Managed Wilderness – Schönefeld Park Landscapes

| 12529 Schönefeld | Area
650,000 m² | **bgmr Landschaftsarchitekten**
www.bgmr.de | Client: Flughafen
Berlin-Brandenburg GmbH |

Wild horses roaming the park In den Gehren

Gabion seating element, In den Gehren

Landscaping of three sites compensating for impacts to the environment resulting from to the construction of BER Airport. These newly created areas of managed
wilderness are located between Berlin's municipal boundary and the airport. The three
reserves comprise half-open spaces whose overall appearance breaks with the con-
ventions of both parks and cultivated landscapes. Groves of trees separate the meadows. Various stations – including gabion seating elements, dunes for climbing, a picnic
meadow, a field of boulders and a lookout – increase the park's recreational value.
A network of pathways spanning seven kilometres connects the reserves with the surrounding districts. Wild horses and heritage cattle are part of the sustainable land
management concept, which uses conservation grazing to maintain the meadows.

Plan detailing all three parks:
Am Vogelwäldchen, Am Dörferblick and
In den Gehren (from top to bottom)

Am Vogelwäldchen and Gropiusstadt

Am Dörferblick (above), Am Vogelwäldchen (below)

Agoraphobia

Where money and history join forces, chances for wide open spaces narrow

*Tempelhofer Feld (left),
Marienkirche in Berlin-Mitte (above)*

In his novel *Wach [Awake]*, Albrecht Selge's insomniac hero August Kreutzer wanders through Berlin at night, past little local bars, urban wastelands, windswept corners, indoor markets, shopping streets. August knows a lot about spending money: by day, he's the manager of a mall. "The mall at lunchtime on a weekday is a world out of balance, as though all the men have disappeared after some great war," he muses. Empty shopping centres are as unbearable as empty city centres.

It's a beautiful idea: the city seen through the eyes of a nightwalker. Selge's 2011 debut novel marked the return of the *flâneur* to contemporary literature, though his Berlin is very different from those of his fellow wanderers Franz Hessel and Walter Benjamin. Selge's Berlin is not feisty and full of life. It is remote, with lots of empty spaces left to the imagination. You can't sit back and absorb Selge's Berlin: you have to fill its voids. As one reviewer in *Die Zeit* put it, Selge's city is a daring venture.

Berlin journalist Klaus Hartung is another *flâneur*. During the 1980s, he revelled in the aesthetics of ruins, wastelands and empty spaces that travel guides still tend to praise. But when the Berlin Wall fell, Hartung lost the courage to explore the voids. "When I stood in front of the Marienkirche for the first time after the Berlin Wall came down, I felt a phantom pain. This is the centre of Berlin, I thought, and neither it nor its history exist any longer."

Ever since then Hartung has campaigned for the gaps to be filled, and particularly the large open area between the Fernsehturm and the Spree. "Every European city has a historic district as the central focus of its identity," he writes, arguing that the new city should be rebuilt on the traces of the old. "Every new generation must decide whether to let its historical memories fade away, or restore them to life."

Hartung is right to point out the many losses Berlin has suffered. But does every wound inflicted by war have to be an empty space, especially if it has been repaired using modern resources? If we mend the present for future generations, must we also mend the past simply because our *horror vacui* cannot tolerate emptiness in the middle of a city?

Architectural sociologist Harald Bodenschatz believes the debate should not simply focus on the Rathausforum, the area between the Fernsehturm, the Spree, the Rotes Rathaus and the Marienkirche. As an enthusiastic participant in this debate, he believes it should include the entire Mitte district, all the way from the new Humboldt Forum to Alexanderplatz and from the Mühlendamm to the Molkenmarkt. Bodenschatz believes that Mitte needs a development plan of its own.

But what should its priorities be? Bodenschatz says there are two main issues: on the one hand preserving the district's history, from its "modest middle-class beginnings" to absolutism, the empire of the Kaisers, and the Weimar Republic, and on the other overcoming the automotive city. The latter concept prevailed in the most recent era of Mitte's history, when it was radically rebuilt first by the Nazis and then by East Germany. "That's when all the open spaces and wasteland appeared, (...) and when the area was redeveloped to accommodate cars." What we're suffering from

right now, Bodenschatz says, is not so much *horror vacui* as *horror urbis*.

Léonie Baumann, the rector of the Berlin Weissensee School of Art, doesn't think the area around the Fernsehturm reflects a fear of the city. "I think it would be creepy to recreate the old Berlin here," she says. "This is obviously driven by a wish to erase the traces of an embarrassing period in our history."

Baumann also questions which period of history a reconstructed city should be based on. Should it be Berlin's six hundred years as a people's city, as advocated by Bodenschatz, or the second half of the twentieth century that Baumann herself refers to? Another obvious question is whether the city can be repaired at all and, if so, whether its history can be made visible again.

She believes the key question is not what we should build in the city, but how we should use it. "I don't see the Fernsehturm as an empty space needing to be filled," she emphasises. "The place is full of people. It's green." Rather, she regards the planned development as an attempt to get rid of East German architecture and its different use of space. "History and money are joining forces to turn a noncommercial place back into a commercial one," she says.

This may also be true of the Tempelhofer Feld. The 360-hectare former airport, now a hugely popular park, has long been a symbol of an untamed and anarchic use of open space, but with a discipline of its own. Its grass and runways are hosts to a diversity of people and lifestyles that many areas of the city have long since lost. The importance of this public place to the people of Berlin was apparent in the May 2014 referendum, when over 60 percent voted against building on it. Here again, as in Mitte, the debate was about whether the area should be public or private. The only difference was that the opponents of development could hardly be accused of trying to sweep history under the carpet, since they called for the remains of the former forced labour camp on the site to be turned into a memorial.

The controversial Rathausforum (left),
the popular Tempelhofer Feld (below)

So it makes a lot of sense to take a critical look at the role of history in the city's development, and question the controversy about its future. When Hartung, Bodenschatz and others use history as an argument, it's always about lost historical heritage and identity. The usual response is that critical reconstruction compensates for lost heritage and identity and gives us back the city. But sometimes the past is rebuilt as a shopping mall, a private commercial space attracting tourists rather than the people who live in the city. That's unless the person doing the building plans to use it themselves, which is what Hartung advocates. Society as a whole should benefit from the reclaiming of the old city, not just investors, with the lost past being reinvented using modern resources.

There are good reasons to doubt this vision. While sites like the Humboldt Forum combine past and present into something new and exciting, this is not going to happen in Mitte, simply because the money is not there. Instead of letting the alliance of money and history have their way, how about backing up community and the present instead? Why shouldn't the city convene and converse in wide open spaces? Why no agoras? And whence this agoraphobia? Could it be that a whole society,

and its ageing champions, are merely projecting their mental instabilities onto the city and its centre?

Another *flâneur*, actor and author Hanns Zischler, takes a much wider view of the city. His often idiosyncratic observations are recorded in his book *Berlin ist zu groß für Berlin [Berlin is too big for Berlin]*. "I don't think there's a great yearning for Berlin to have a single centre." It has always had more than one, and "this will always be an asset." So he makes no mention of the former old city, instead concentrating on places that have often been labelled as empty urban wastelands, such as the Berliner Kulturforum, which he criticises primarily for blocking Alte Potsdamer Strasse.

"[When Hans] Scharoun made the grand gesture of building the Staatsbibliothek on this street, he severed a historically and geographically important artery," Zischler says. He believes the city was being made a scapegoat, an effect reinforced by its division by plans for an autobahn in West Berlin. The Staatsbibliothek site was intended to shield Scharoun's Kulturforum from the noise of the autobahn to be built behind the library, though this never materialised. Here, the *horror vacui* is literally tangible.

But what do you do with a space like this? It took away Berlin's historic boundaries, and the idea of a *Stadtlandschaft*, or 'urban landscape', was a deliberate counterpart to the densely built city of the nineteenth century, which had no empty spaces, but only squares, intersections and parks.

Zischler very much liked the design by Portuguese architect Álvaro Siza, who proposed banishing traffic from the Kulturforum as a way of countering the *horror vacui* and perhaps allowing Berliners finally to regain possession of their city.

Ordinary people – and not: consumers – as the driving force behind urban development policy: it's an attractive idea that could render redundant the whole question of how to deal with Berlin's past and future. But it's not an easy concept to come to terms with, as the insomniac hero of Albrecht Selge's *Wach* discovers. "August has ended up in a big open space. He was heading this way anyway, but this is the kind of big open space you end up in without meaning to. No matter how densely populated, it always seems empty. It's miles of urban desert, steppe and scrapyard all in one, a desolate landscape of concrete slabs, isolated buildings, water features, ramps, patches of embattled greenery, long lines of apartment blocks stretching away to the horizon."

Tree remains at the Kulturforum (above left),
trees are thin on the ground at Tempelhof (above)

Gartenstadt Drewitz

Konrad-Wolf-Allee
14480 Potsdam

Planning area
400,000 m²

**Stadt · Land · Fluss, Büro für
Städtebau und Stadtplanung BDA SRL**
www.slf-berlin.de

Client: City of Potsdam
and ProPotsdam GmbH

Konrad-Wolf-Allee Park

A fountain in the new park

Improving energy efficiency and revitalising an estate – a collaborative project with Pia von Zadow Landschaftsarchitekten, Projektkommunikation Hagenau, Dr. Brenner Ingenieurgesellschaft and Merkel Ingenieure Consult. Drewitz housing estate is home to more than 5,800 people. Konrad-Wolf-Allee cuts the estate in two. The modification of this thoroughfare is a central component of the project. Much of the oversized roadway has been converted into a predominantly barrier-free park. Parking management and alternative forms of transportation complement the re-organisation of traffic flows. The park, when extended into a "green junction" – is expected to emerge as the estate's new centre. In 2014 the estate's CO_2 emissions were down 775 tons from 2009. They are expected to drop by 87 percent by 2050 following the implementation of the proposed measures.

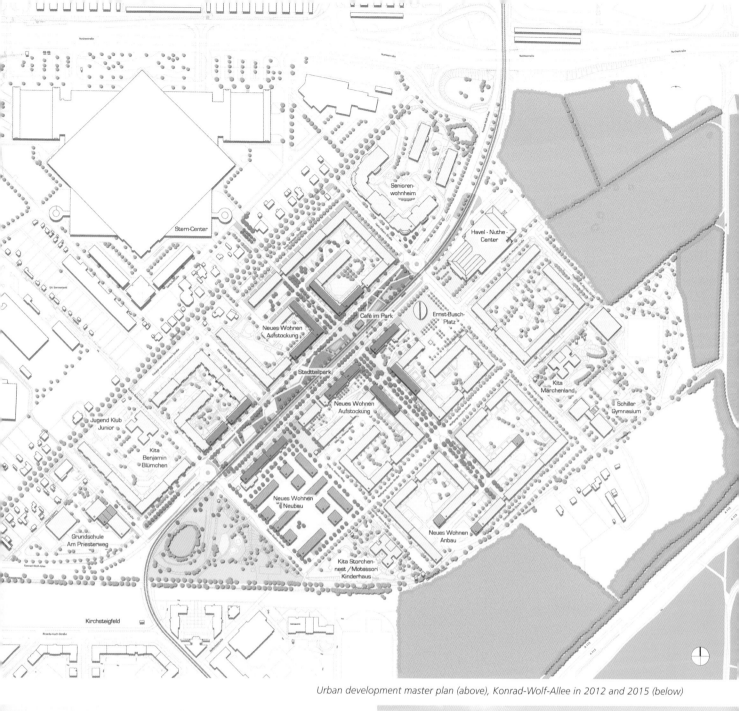

Urban development master plan (above), Konrad-Wolf-Allee in 2012 and 2015 (below)

ISEK Altstadt Spandau

| 13597 Berlin | Planning area 570,000 m² | **Herwarth + Holz, Planung und Architektur** www.herwarth-holz.de | Client: Spandau Borough Council, Berlin |

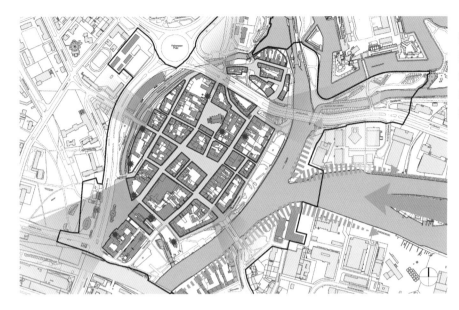

Key aspects

☐ Altstadt character

▨ Urban space as a stage

▨ Access ways

⊷ Spree-Havel revitalisation

✳ Altstadt as a community space

Spandau's historic centre and St. Nicholas Church

Measures

Upgrading of public roads ☐

Redevelopment of public spaces ▨

Redevelopment measures / conversion ▨

Redevelopment / construction of public areas along the embankment ▨

Targeted / supplementary measures to enhance public green spaces ▤

Re-utilisation / enhancement of key locations ▤

Creation of new bridges ↔

Potential bridge sites (to be clarified) ◄►

Enhancement of bridge sites ⊏ ⊐

Boundary of area approved for funding for the preservation of urban sites of historic interest ▭

The integrated urban development concept (ISEK) identifies the opportunities, objectives and measures for the long-term development of Spandau's historic centre. The concept outlines a process of long-term revitalisation spanning social and economic development, urban planning, environmental planning and transportation infrastructure. Key issues include the area's character, the role of urban space as a stage, access, the revitalisation of the Spree-Havel embankment, and the centre as a community space. The adoption of the ISEK is the basis for the borough's admission to the funding programme for the preservation of urban sites of historic interest. The planning process was conducted in dialogue with the authorities, citizens and relevant actors at the local level. This dialogue invited stakeholders to share their views on- and offline, and included citizen forums and an exhibition.

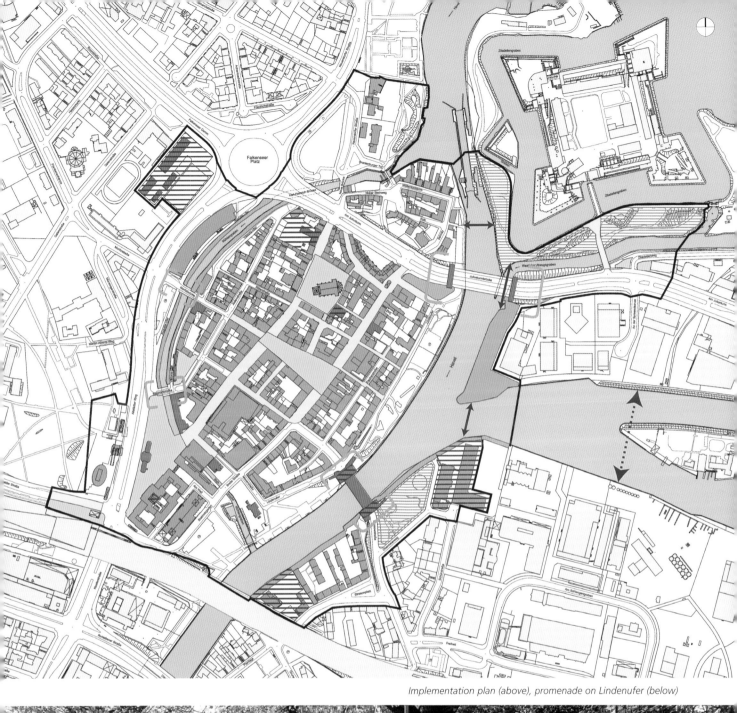

Implementation plan (above), promenade on Lindenufer (below)

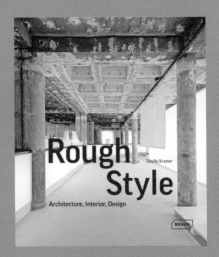

Rough Style

Rough Style – Architecture, Interior, Design
ISBN 978-3-03768-195-4

€ 59,95

Black +
Architecture

Black + Architecture
ISBN 978-3-03768-199-2

€ 49,90

XS

XS – small houses big time
ISBN 978-3-03768-202-9

€ 44,90

BRAUN

braun-publishing.ch

Architects

Authors

Louis Back

born 1963, studied Communications and Cultural Studies in Munich and Detroit. Freelance journalist and author specialising in architecture, garden design, environmental issues and urban planning. Editor of *Building Berlin* since 2007

Cornelia Dörries

born 1969, studied Sociology in Berlin and Manchester. Freelance journalist and author in the fields of architecture, interior design, landscape architecture, urban development and urban history. Editor of the magazine *Deutsches Architektenblatt* since 2010

Oliver G. Hamm

born 1963, studied Architecture in Darmstadt. From 1989 through to 2009, editor (*db, Bauwelt*) and editor-in-chief (*VfA Profil, polis, Deutsches Architektenblatt, greenbuilding*). His work has been published in numerous books. He lives in Berlin and works as a freelance author, publisher, editor and curator

Simone Hübener

born 1980, studied Architecture in Karlsruhe and Rome. She works as a freelance journalist for industry publications and book publishers

Falk Jaeger

born 1950, studied Architecture and Art History, and is a Professor of Architecture Theory. He lives in Berlin and works as a freelance architecture critic, curator and journalist

Friederike Meyer

born 1972, studied Architecture in Aachen and Seattle, Art History in Dresden, and Journalism in Berlin. An editor of the magazine *Bauwelt* since 2000, she has published books and articles on architecture and urban planning

Uwe Rada

born 1963, studied German and History. He has been an editor at the German national daily newspaper *die tageszeitung* since 1992. He is the author of several books, including *Hauptstadt der Verdrängung* (1997) and *Berliner Barbaren* (2001)

Frank Seehausen

born 1971, studied Architecture and Art History in Berlin and lives and works as an architect, author and lecturer in Berlin and Braunschweig. Since 2013 lecturer on the history of urban mobility at TU Berlin's Center for Metropolitan Studies, author of diverse publications on post-war architecture

Photo Credits

AFF Architekten: p. 29 (top) – **Mark Asipowicz:** front cover (bottom centre), p. 64, 65 – **Bettina Bergande:** p. 160, 161 (top) – **bgmr Landschaftsarchitekten:** p. 166 – **Jan Bitter:** p. 36 (right), 37 – **Jens Boesenberg:** p. 50, 51 – **Ulf Böttcher:** p. 175 (left) – **Luftbild Bollmann Bildkarten-Verlag:** p. 140 (right) – **bpk/Kunstbibliothek SMB/Dietmar Katz:** p. 9 – **Alexander Paul Brandes:** p. 156 (top), 157 (top) – **Zooey Braun:** p. 58, 59 – **Marcus Bredt:** front cover (top left), p. 104, 105 – **Celia de Coca:** p. 118, 119 – **Stefan Dauth:** p. 12, 13 – **Marcus Ebener:** front cover (centre left), p. 140 (right), 141 – **Alberto Ferreira:** p. 56, 57 – **Thilo Folkerts:** p. 158, 159 – **Andreas Friedel/Christoph Naumann:** p.22, 23 – **Bernhard Friese:** p. 138, 139 – **Christian Gahl:** p. 86, 87 – **gbp Architekten:** p. 49 (bottom right) – **Luca Girardini:** p. 60, 61 – **Brigida Gonzalez:** front cover (bottom left), p. 142, 143 – **Tomek Goździewicz/Wikimedia Commons:** p. 149 – **Klaus Graubner:** p. 30, 31 – **Bernadette Grimmenstein:** p. 72, 73 – **Roland Halbe:** p. 54, 55 – **Axel Hartmann:** p. 120, 121 – **Oliver Heinl:** p. 102, 103 – **Lv Hengzhong:** front cover (centre right), p. 122, 123 – **Herwarth + Holz:** p. 176, 177 – **hiepler, brunier,:** p. 146, 147 – **Allard van der Hoek:** p. 62, 63 – **Florian Holzherr:** p. 145 (bottom) – **Hüffer.Ramin:** p. 90, 91 – **Werner Huthmacher:** p. 18, 19, 24, 25, 68, 69, 98, 99, 110, 111, 114, 115, 124, 125, 128, 129 – **Hanns Joosten:** p. 92 (left), 93 (bottom left and right), 151 (top), 154, 155, 164, 165 – **Nikolay Kazakov:** p. 52, 53 – **Carsten Krohn:** p. 16, 17 – **Andreas Labes:** p. 80, 81 – **léonwohlhage:** p. 14 (top right), 15 (bottom) – **Florian Licht:** p. 84 (top) – **Linus Lintner:** p. 116, 117 – **Olaf Mahlstedt:** p. 130, 131 – **Benjamin Maltry:** back cover (centre), p. 174 – **Eva Mayer-Laipple:** p. 42, 43 – **Andreas Meichsner:** p. 82, 85, 126, 127 – **Simon Menges:** p. 20, 21, 40, 41 – **Tom Mival:** p. 36 (left) – **Sorin Morar:** back cover (top), p. 34, 35 – **Frank Müller:** p. 93 (top) – **Stefan Müller:** p. 66, 67 – **Michael Nagy/Presseamt München:** p. 152 – **Gernot Nalbach:** p. 96, 97 – **nARCHITECTS:** p. 10 – **nARCHITECTS/mir.no:** p. 11 (top) – **Markus Nass/Arena Berlin:** p. 84 (bottom) – **Nedelykov Moreira Architekten:** p. 144, 145 (top) – **Erik-Jan Ouwerkerk:** p. 11 (bottom), 44, 45, 46, 47, 74, 76, 77, 83, 106, 107, 109, 134, 135, 136, 137, 148, 150, 151 (bottom), 168, 169, 170, 171, 172, 173 – **PARTNERUNDPARTNER Architekten:** p. 94, 95 – **Quabbe & Tessmann:** p. 32, 33 (top) – **realities:united:** p. 153 – **Christian Richters:** p. 132, 133 – **Christian Rose:** p. 8, 88, 89 – **Thomas Rosenthal:** p. 167 – **Christian Schink:** p. 28, 29 (bottom) – **Cordia Schlegelmilch:** p. 26, 27 – **Ulrich Schwarz:** front cover (bottom right), p. 38, 39 – **Mark Seelen:** p. 48, p. 49 (top and bottom left) – **Adam Stevens:** p. 175 (right) – **Nina Straßgütl:** p. 70, 71, 100, 101, 112, 113 – **Joachim Swillus:** p. 92 (right) – **TRU Architekten:** p. 33 (bottom) – **ullstein bild/Fritz Eschen:** p. 75 – **Udo Walgenbach:** p. 161 (bottom) – **Roland Weegen/GEWOFAG:** p. 14 (top left), 15 (top) – **Philip JSF Winkelmeyer:** back cover (bottom), p. 162, 163 – **Thomas Wolf:** p. 157 (bottom) – **Ute Zscharnt:** front cover (top right), p. 78, 79

Copyright for the art installation p. 145: James Turrell

All rights to unbuilt designs, floor plans and other graphic representations not listed above are property of the respective architectural firms.

The Deutsche Nationalbibliothek lists this publication in the Deutsche Nationalbibliografie; detailed bibliographic data are available in the internet at http://dnb.dnb.de.

ISBN 978-3-03768-205-0
ISSN 1439-927X

1st edition 2016
Published by the Berlin Chamber of Architects

Project Selection
Dipl.-Ing. Volker Auch-Schwelk, architect, Stuttgart
Prof. Mag. Arch. Carlo Baumschlager, architect, Dornbirn (Austria)
Dipl.-Ing. Nikolaus Börn, interior architect, Hamburg
Dipl.-Ing. Irene Burkhardt, landscape architect, Munich
Dipl.-Ing. Sabine Feldmann, urban planner, Düsseldorf
Sascha Hingst, editor and television presenter, Berlin
Dipl.-Ing. Gerold Reker, architect, Kaiserslautern

Chief Editor
Louis Back

Editorial Coordination
Birgit Koch, Meike Capatti
in cooperation with committees of the Berlin Chamber of Architects

Translation
www.networktranslators.de

Layout
Ben Buschfeld, buschfeld.com – graphic and interface design